A Practical Guide to Personal Injuries in Sport

Adam Walker
LLB Hons, PGDip
Clinical Negligence, Personal Injury, Sports Law and Inquests

Patricia Leonard
BCL (Hons) (NUI), BCL (Oxon)
Clinical Negligence, Personal Injury and Sports Law

Barristers at 7 Bedford Row

Law Brief Publishing

Published 2016 by
Law Brief Publishing
30 The Parks
Minehead
Somerset
TA24 8BT

www.lawbriefpublishing.com

Paperback: 978-1-911035-04-6

To Lucia

and

To Mark

PREFACE

"It is said that there is no authority as to what is the standard of care which covers the conduct of players in competitive sports generally and, above all, in a competitive sport whose rules and general background contemplate that there will be physical contact between the players but that appears to be the position ... It is not for me in this court to define exhaustively the duty of care between players in a football game."

Lord Donaldson MR, *Condon v Basi*[1]

Sport has become increasingly commercialised, which has in turn led to an increase in the financial stakes for participants and clubs in particular and greater financial loss should a participant suffer injury. As a result, there has been a significant increase in recourse to the courts when things go badly. Parties seek new and inventive ways to recover damages from a variety of sources for injuries sustained in the sporting context. The area of negligence in sport has moved a long way since 1985[2] when it was observed that there was no reported authority as to the applicable standard of care.

Within the realm of sports law more generally, as contrasted with sports law in the personal injury context, this area has developed a jurisprudence of its own and indeed now has its own tribunals[3] and means of dispute resolution.

While in the personal injury context liability is firmly grounded in general principles that are equally applicable to the non-sports personal injury case, some issues feature more prominently in the sporting arena and as such deserve closer consideration and analysis. In particular, it is necessary to consider why it is that demonstrating liability for injury in the sporting context is generally more difficult than in other areas of personal injury law notwithstanding that it has been acknowledged throughout the case law that sports men and women are just as entitled

---

1 [1985] 1 WLR 866, the first reported English case involving participator violence.

2 Condon v Basi (above).

3 E.g. the Court of Arbitration for Sport.

to the protection of the law from unnecessary injury brought about by negligent or reckless conduct on (and, in some circumstances, off) the sporting field, even where one is concerned with contact sports or other sports involving very significant inherent risks. What has been clearly identified within the case law is the need to balance the interest of the public in sports with considerations of safety and participant and spectator protection.[4]

When considering liability for injury in the sporting context, basic concepts such as whether a duty of care is owed and, if so, what the appropriate standard of care may be, require particular attention. A discussion of issues such as the effect of recent case law on the area of vicarious liability and the use of the defence of *volenti non fit injuria* within cases dealing with sports that involve inherent risks of injury, is also necessary. While it has been said in this area that *"the court has to find the facts, apply the law and that is the end of it"*,[5] complexities do arise in many aspects of sporting cases, as has been recognised in many other works,[6] including in respect of questions such as whether or not negligence can simply be inferred from the facts and whether a breach of duty arises in the case of, *"mere errors of judgment"*,[7] particularly when conduct that would be sanctioned on the street, may be deemed acceptable on the sports field.

The general principles in respect of liability in negligence, trespass to the person and contract are discussed in the first two chapters when considering the liability of the sporting competitor or participant to other participants and to spectators. Later chapters consider the liability of those responsible for the sporting venue, of the event promoter or organiser, of the sports official, of the sporting governing body or licensing authority and also that of the sports physician, while the available defences and the question of the assessment of damages are dealt with in separate chapters. An exposition of the current state of the law relating vicarious liability is dealt with in a separate chapter, as is the subject of abuse in the sports context.

---

4 Grayson, *"Sport & The Law"*, 3rd edition, 1999, Ch. 6.

5 Per Sir Michael Davies in Champion v Brown, unreported, 24 Feb 1993, whose view was also that Condon v Basi [1985] 1 WLR 866 was *"crystal clear"*.

6 E.g. Grayson (above, n.4).

7 Wooldridge v Sumner [1963] 2 QB 43.

Ultimately, it is hoped that this guide will be a useful reference tool for sports lawyers and personal injury practitioners in respect of the sort of issues that they are likely to meet on a regular basis in the course of their busy practice and that it provides an efficient introduction to what points should be considered at the earliest stage.

Adam Walker & Patricia Leonard
7 Bedford Row
September 2016

Contents

CHAPTER ONE
LIABILITY OF THE PLAYER TO OTHER PLAYERS

INTRODUCTION

As national and international interest in and remuneration for participation in sport at the highest levels have increased over the last 50 years or so, so too has the potential financial loss and damage associated with a career-ending injury attributable to the carelessness of fellow participants. That is clearly one reason why the injured player may now, more than ever before, be more likely to consider pursuing an alleged wrongdoer in civil proceedings. Civil liability of one participant to another for damages for personal injury is predominantly based in tort and in particular in negligence and trespass to the person.

This chapter considers the liability of the player or competitor to their fellow participants. It deals with general principles of liability in negligence with particular regard to the questions of duty of care and breach of duty, including discussion of the appropriate standard of care. The chapter goes on to consider a number of cases relevant to these questions and the circumstances in which liability has been established in the reported case law and in contrast, where it has not. Other potential heads of liability are then considered in turn, including liability for assault, in contract and in public and private nuisance.

(1) LIABILITY IN NEGLIGENCE

Background

As with all cases in which negligence at common law is relied upon as a cause of action, a claimant must demonstrate that a duty of care was owed to them by the defendant, that the defendant was in breach of that duty and that as a result of that breach of duty the claimant suffered loss and damage, which loss was not so unforeseeable as to be too remote to be recoverable.[1]

---

1 Clerk & Lindsell on Torts, 21st edition, Chapter 8 at 8-04.

Liability in negligence in the context of involvement in sporting events often has an additional level of complexity however given that in many cases participation necessarily involves the acceptance of a level of risk of injury to the competitor. In contact sports, for example, a risk of injury cannot reasonably be avoided and liability will be made out only where the claimant's injury has arisen because of an additional risk of injury having been introduced by particularly careless participation.[2] Liability in negligence as between players involves a consideration of concepts such as the extent of a participant's consent to or acceptance of a risk of injury and as a natural extension to that consent the defence of *volenti non fit injuria* has been advanced in many cases. Consent and *volenti* are discussed in more detail in chapter 10.

The application of the law of negligence in this area of activity is also complicated by the tension between ensuring that the law recognizes and acknowledges the social utility of sport[3] and the need to give the participant a wide margin of error, but also ensuring that it provides protection to such participants from over exuberant and reckless conduct.

The duty of care

In circumstances where there are multiple participants in a particular sporting activity, the existence of a duty of care in negligence is unlikely to be disputed; it is generally accepted that it is foreseeable that a failure

---

2 A comparison might be drawn here to a claim in negligence in the clinical context in which a patient signs a consent form consenting to a risk of a recognized complication, where that complication arises, but the claimant is able to demonstrate that it did so not due to the general risk of that complication associated with the procedure, but due to a negligent failure.

3 Now expressly acknowledged in section 1 of the Compensation Act 2006 which provides that, *"A court considering a claim in negligent or breach of statutory duty may in determining whether the defendant should have taken particular steps to meet a standard of care (whether by taking precautions against a risk or otherwise) have regard to whether a requirement to take those steps might (a) prevent a desirable activity from being undertaken at all, to a particular extent or in a particular way, or (b) discourage persons from undertaking functions in connection with a desirable activity"*, although this has perhaps always been recognised by the fact that contact sports such as boxing where the likelihood of injury is high are permitted at all.

to take reasonable care when participating in a sporting activity might cause injury to another participant, that fellow participants in sport are sufficiently proximate to each other to ground a duty of care and that it is fair, just and reasonable to impose a duty in those circumstances.[4] The extent of that duty however may be subject to the question of the risks that participants can be taken to have accepted and the duty requires that players exercise the degree of care appropriate to the circumstances.[5]

Breach of duty and the standard of care

Generally speaking the question of what was expected in the circumstances is considered at the breach of duty stage when setting the appropriate standard of care against which the actions of the defendant are to be measured. The standard of care is objective in that the test for the court is whether the defendant's actions have fallen below the conduct of a reasonably competent player of that sport. The standard is based on the activity being undertaken and does not take account of the particular features of the defendant. However the court will take account of the competitive nature of the sport and what is reasonably to be expected in that particular sporting activity. In some cases the court has also had regard to the level of skill of the participants under consideration, to aid in the setting of the appropriate standard of care.[6]

Unsurprisingly, it has been acknowledged by the courts in countless cases that the nature of sporting activity is such that decisions are often taken in the heat of the moment and in order to take account of that reality liability has said to arise where injury has resulted only from an,

---

4 Caparo Industries plc v Dickman [1990] 2 AC 605 applying Donoghue v Stevenson [1932] AC 562.

5 See Sir John Donaldson MR in Condon v Basi [1985] 1 WLR 866 at 867F, citing a passage of Chief Justice Barwick in Rootes v Shelton [1968] ALR 33, although the Court of Appeal in Condon v Basi preferred the view of Kitto J. in Rootes v Shelton, that there is a general duty to take reasonable care, which is fact specific and which one considers at the breach of duty stage.

6 In Condon v Basi (supra, n.5) Sir John Donaldson MR observed that, *"...there will of course be a higher degree of care required of a player in a First Division football match than of a player in a Fourth Division football match"* at 868F-G.

"error of judgment that a reasonable competitor ... would not have made",[7] as contrasted with a *"mere error of judgment"*.

While in the reported case law one sees various different tests having been applied, including whether the act complained of amounted only to a *"mere error of judgment"*[8] or whether the conduct complained of showed a *"reckless disregard"* for the safety of other players, the test applied most consistently and the one which represents the present state of the law is to ask whether reasonable care was taken in all of the circumstances. In the leading case of Condon v Basi,[9] a footballer was held to have acted negligently in the manner in which he went into a tackle with the consequence that the tackled player sustained a fractured leg. Sir John Donaldson MR applied a similar test of reasonable care, stating that, *"...there is a general standard of care ... that you are under a duty to take all reasonable care taking account of the circumstances in which you are placed, which, in a game of football, are quite different from those which affect you when you are going for a walk in the countryside"*. The Court of Appeal upheld the judgment of the judge at first instance who had found the defendant to have been, *"clearly guilty ... of serious and dangerous foul play which showed a reckless disregard of the Plaintiff's safety and which fell far below the standards which might reasonably be expected in anyone pursuing the game"*, but it was not suggested that *"reckless disregard"* for the safety other participants was the benchmark to be applied.[10] Subsequently, in Smoldon v Whitworth & Nolan,[11] the suggestion that a claimant must prove recklessness was rejected in the context of a claim brought by a rugby player against a referee for damages for injury sustained as a result of a collapsed scrummage. The level of care required was said to be, *"that which is appropriate in all the circumstances, and the circumstances are of crucial importance"*. It was

7 Wilks v Cheltenham Homeguard Motor Cycle & Light Car Club [1971] 1 WLR 668.

8 E.g. as in Caldwell v Maguire [2001] EWCA Civ 1054.

9 Supra n.5.

10 That test had been applied however in a number of cases following Wooldridge v Sumner [1963] 2 QB 43, Wilks (supra n.7) and Harrison v Vincent [1982] RTR 8.

11 [1997] PIQR P133, CA.

observed that there will be no liability for errors of judgment, oversights or lapses of which any participant might be guilty in the context of a fast moving and vigorous contest.

The test formulated in Condon v Basi was also applied in Caldwell v Maguire,[12] which confirmed that there will be no liability for mere errors of judgment or lapses during the course of the contest. In that case a professional jockey was injured in the course of a race as a result of a horse veering across his path as a result of two other riders' actions, which were determined by the Jockey Club's stewards to have been careless riding and in breach of Jockey Club Rules. It was held that there would be no liability for lapses in judgment in the context of a fast moving contest or in the heat and commitment of the race. While the Jockey Club's stewards had made findings of reckless riding they were not conclusive of liability in negligence at common law.

At first instance it was held that each participant owes a duty of care to other participants, that the duty was to exercise all care that was objectively reasonable in the prevailing circumstances to avoid inflicting injury, that the *"prevailing circumstances"* are all such circumstances that are properly attendant on the contest and they include its object, the demands inevitably made upon its contestants, its inherent dangers, its rules, conventions and customs, and the standards of skill and judgment to be reasonably expected of a contestant. It was said that the threshold for liability in practice is high and that proof of a breach of duty will not come from demonstrating a mere error of judgment or a momentary lapse in skill and care when subject to stresses of a race.[13] Finally, it was observed that in practice it would be difficult to prove breach of duty in absence of conduct that amounts to reckless disregard for another contestant's safety. The Court of Appeal reviewed a series of earlier cases,[14] held that Condon and Smoldon were binding and that

12 [2001] EWCA Civ 1054.

13 As had already been observed by Lord Bingham LCJ, in Smoldon v Whitworth & Nolan [1997] PIQR P133.

14 Including Condon (supra, n.5), Wooldridge [1963] 2 QB 43 (reckless disregard – spectator), Wilks v Cheltenham Homeguard Motor Cycle Co & Light Car Cycle Club [1971] 1 WLR 668 (reckless disregard – spectator), Harrison v Vincent (ordinary standard applied regarding injury due to defective brakes) and Smoldon

the reference to *"reckless disregard"* was no more than a reference to the practicalities of proving a breach of duty on the facts of some cases and was not a statement that that was the appropriate legal test to be applied. Judge LJ commented that it was correct to state that the threshold is often high and that the circumstances of the case are of crucial importance.

Accordingly, it now appears clear that the test when considering breach of duty is not one of reckless disregard for safety, but rather is one of whether there has been a failure to take such care as was reasonable in the prevailing circumstances, with the facts and circumstances being of utmost importance. While there have been references to the facts and circumstances impacting on the nature and extent of the duty of care, the position since Condon has been that the preferred approach is that there is a general duty of care owed as between participants and the facts and circumstances are matters that should be considered at the breach of duty stage.

Circumstances relevant to the question of breach of duty

As to the features relevant for the court to consider when setting the standard of care and in determining whether the standard of care has or has not been met, the court has identified as relevant features the nature of the sport under consideration and its inherent risks; the nature of the defendant's actions; whether the injury was caused in the heat of the moment or during strenuous competition; the age and skill of the competitors; whether sporting rules or conventions had been broken and the cost/difficulty associated with the taking of precautions.

The nature of the particular sport in question

Whether the sport is a contact or a non-contact sport will clearly inform the question of the acceptability of a participant's actions but a perhaps more subtle question is that of the nature of the risks inherent in the sport under consideration. As is identified by Beloff et al., clearly different standards should apply to boxing and rugby as compared with

---

(supra, n.13).

crown green bowls.[15] In some cases the nature and extent of the risks to be expected will be obvious whereas in others expert evidence may be required.

The conduct under consideration

Obviously the action or conduct of the defendant will be considered as the basis of the complaint, however the court will take account of the risks associated with that action and whether such risks would or should have been obvious to the defendant.

Age of the competitor

The age of competitor is relevant at the point at which breach of duty is being considered. While the standard of care is still objective the child participant may be able to prey in aid the fact that a feature of all similar participants was a lesser capacity for foresight and prudence.[16]

Skill of the participant

The decision in Condon perhaps suggests that higher standards of care are owed by professional participants than by amateurs.[17] It has been noted in other texts however that the observation was *obiter*, is not consistent with the law of negligence more generally[18] and that it may lead to anomalous results, e.g. in circumstances where a professional team plays an amateur team different participants would be held to different standards of care.[19] In a number of cases the preferred position has been that the standard is the same for the amateur and the professional,

---

15 Beloff et. al., *Sports Law*, Second Edition, 2012, p142 at 5.43.

16 Kitto J. in McHale v Watson (1966) 115 CLR.

17 In Condon v Basi (supra, n.5) Sir John Donaldson MR observed that, *"..there will of course be a higher degree of care required of a player in a First Division football match than of a player in a Fourth Division football match"* at 868F-G.

18 See in particular Nettleship v Weston [1971] 2 QB 691 in which it was confirmed that a learner driver is held to the same standard as a qualified driver.

19 Beloff et.al., Sports Law, 2nd edition 2012, p143 at 5.45 and Kevan et. al., Sports Personal Injury: Law and Practice, 2002, p40 at 3.23.

i.e. that of the reasonable professional contestant.[20] It was observed in Vowles v Evans,[21] that in Smoldon there had been inconclusive discussion as to the effect of the grade of the defendant referee and Lord Phillips MR concluded in Vowles that on the particular facts of the case it did not matter but that there was *"scope for argument"* on the question.[22] In Smoldon, Lord Bingham LCJ had stated that the distinction did not matter on the facts of the case but the plaintiff's formulation was preferred, *viz.* that the standard to which the referee was to be held should depend not on his grade but on the function he was purporting to perform.[23] As has been noted elsewhere the position still remains somewhat unclear.[24]

Heat of the moment

As has been discussed above it was confirmed in Smoldon and Caldwell that there will be no liability for errors of judgment, oversights or lapses during a fast moving contest. However, different considerations have been said to apply in circumstances where injury has resulted from a negligent failure to prepare for the competition or during quiet passages of play as contrasted with errors in decision-making in the heat of the competition, when there has been no or very limited time in which to consider the action being criticized.[25] In cases where negligent planning has brought about the injury there is no question of the decision under criticism having been made in the heat and commitment of the contest.

---

20 E.g. as in Elliott v Saunders & Liverpool FC, unreported, 10 Jun 1994, (1) Gordon Watson & (2) Bradford City AFC (1983) Ltd v (1) Kevin Gray & Huddersfield Town AFC, Times, Nov 26, 1998, LTL 6/11/98 and Pitcher v Huddersfield Town Football Club Ltd, QBD, July 17, 2001.

21 [2003] EWCA Civ 318.

22 At para 28.

23 See Smoldon [1997] PIQR P133 at 139.

24 Kevan et. al, Sports Personal Injury: Law and Practice, 2002, at p51, 3.39.

25 E.g. see Harrison v Vincent [1982] RTR 8.

Whether the rules of the sport were complied with

In Condon v Basi, it was confirmed that the question of whether the rules of the sport in question have been complied with is a relevant consideration but it is not determinative.[26] Lord Donaldson MR cited with approval a passage from the judgment of Kitto J. in the Australian case of Rootes v Shelton[27] in which it was stated that, *"non-compliance with such rules is necessarily one consideration to be attended to upon the question of reasonableness; but it is only one, and it may be that much or little or even no weight in the circumstances."* There have been many decided cases in which compliance or non-compliance with sporting rules and regulations have been a predominant consideration however.[28] Indeed, Beloff has observed[29] that while the observations made in Rootes and Condon in respect of sporting rules not being determinative of liability may be correct, with sports such as rugby and football, it will in practice be almost impossible to establish liability without also demonstrating a breach of the rules of the game.

Cost/availability of precautions

As in any case of negligence it may be relevant that a defendant would have been put to particular cost or expense in steps to guard against injury. In the sports context this might arise at the planning stage, prior to commencement of the competition.[30]

---

26 See Lord Donaldson MR at 868A-C.

27 [1968] ALR 33.

28 In Wright v Cheshire CC [1952] 2 All ER 789, the Court of Appeal overturned a liability decision against a defendant in respect of injury arising from gymnastic activities on the basis that the criticized conduct was in compliance with generally accepted practice and see also Gilsenan v Gunning (1982) 137 DLR 3d 252 (customs of the slopes relied upon in determining liability for a skiing accident), Leatherland v Edwards, unreported, 28 Oct 1998, (defendant in breach of safety rule intrinsic to uni-hockey) and cases referred to by Grayson, *Sport & the Law*, 3rd edition, 1999, at 278.

29 Beloff et. al., *Sports Law*, 2nd edition, 2012, p142 at para 5.42.

30 As in Harrison v Vincent (supra n.25) and in Lewis v Bucknall Golf Club [1993] CLT (Sh Ct) 43, in which the defendant failed to wait before driving off 5th tee, injuring the pursuer.

Burden of proof

As with any claim in negligence it is for the claimant to discharge the burden of proof on the balance of probabilities.[31] While in other claims in negligence it might be open to a claimant to prey in aid the evidential principle of *res ipsa loquitur*, or that *"the facts [of the accident or injury] speak for themselves"* and invite an inference of negligence to be drawn from the fact of the accident or injury, that is unlikely to be of much use to a claimant in the context of an injury resulting from the carelessness of participants in sport as in many cases the sport in question will involve an inherent degree of risk and the fact of injury will therefore not be sufficient of itself to raise a *prima facie* case of negligence. The claimant must demonstrate that the injury resulted not from the non-negligent exposure to risk, but to the increased risk associated with a participant's carelessness. The position might be different of course in relation to sports that ought to involve no or very limited risk of injury, e.g. crown green bowls.

Remoteness of damage

In relation to the liability of one participant to another issues of remoteness of damage rarely arise. Provided that some damage of a particular kind is foreseeable to the claimant's person then the claimant may recover damages for the full extent of that damage, notwithstanding that the extent or the way in which the damage was caused was unforeseeable. The courts have generally taken a wide approach in claims for damages for personal injury to the question of whether the nature of the damage was reasonably foreseeable.[32]

---

31 An exception exists however in circumstances where the defendant's conduct that is the subject of the civil claim has also resulted in him/her being convicted of an offence. In those circumstances the burden is reversed by operation of s.11 of the Civil Evidence Act 1968. The fact of the conviction is taken as proof of commission of the offence unless the contrary is proved.

32 Hughes v Lord Advocate [1963] AC 837 and Bradford v Robinson Rentals [1967] 1 WLR 337.

Illustrations of liability

Liability has been demonstrated in the following circumstances:

(a) Where a footballer performed a dangerous tackle.[33]

(b) Where a motorcycle rider was responsible for a brake failure due to errors prior to the start of a race, causing injury to his sidecar passenger.[34]

(c) Where a hockey player was injured as a result of a high follow-through by another player.[35]

(d) Where a water skier was injured when he collided with a stationary boat due to the conduct of the boat driver.[36]

Liability was not been established in these circumstances:

(1) Where a footballer was injured by another player, when both had reached the ball at the same time and where the tackle was adjudged not to have been a foul or late.[37]

(2) Where a footballer had mis-timed a tackle and made an error of judgment but nothing more.[38]

(3) Where a rugby player sued a player on the opposing side for collapsing a scrum.[39]

---

33 Condon v Basi (supra), McCord v Swansea City AFC & Cornforth (1996) QBD, 19 December 1996, Watson v Bradford City Association FC (1983) Ltd (1998) QBD, 29 October 1998, Rollason v Matthews (2006) Bristol CC, 31 Jan 2006, LTL 2/6/2006.

34 Harrison v Vincent (supra, n.25).

35 Leatherland v Edwards, 28 October 1998, QBD, Newman J., Lawtel 23/1/99.

36 Rootes v Shelton [1968] ALR 33 (HC, Aus)

37 Kerr v Willis [2009] EWCA Civ 1248.

38 Pitcher v Huddersfield Town FC Ltd, 17 Jul 2001, QBD, Hallett J. and Elliott v Saunders, 10 Jun 1994, QBD, unreported.

39 Smoldon v Whitworth [1997] ELR 115 (QBD) and 249 (CA).

(4) A sidecar passenger's claim against the motorcycle rider for injuries sustained during a race, due to having missed a gear.[40]

(2) LIABILITY FOR TRESPASS TO THE PERSON

A participant may also be liable to another participant for the civil wrong of trespass to the person and in more specifically in the tort of battery, the intentional or reckless infliction of unlawful physical contact. In Letang v Cooper,[41] it was suggested by Lord Denning MR that assault was confined to cases where the infliction of contact was deliberate and negligence to circumstances where there was no intention, however intention to cause injury or damage is not an absolute requirement of the tort of battery as it may be made out where the perpetrator is reckless as to whether their use of force will result in injury.[42] There is therefore a degree of overlap between trespass and negligence to that extent although a claimant is unlikely to find themselves in any better position by pleading their case in trespass rather than in negligence. While trespass is actionable *per se* and as such does not require the claimant to prove physical harm to make out an actionable claim, the reason that the claim will have been brought at all will have been to enable the claimant to recover damages for their injury. As such the claimant will have to prove the nature of his or her injury and its extent in any event. However an assault may be established even if it results from a misjudgment by a player or where perpetrated in the *"heat of the moment"*.

As a battery is inflicted on the imposition of unlawful contact and the acceptance of or the giving of consent to physical contact renders that contact lawful, in circumstances where a defendant can demonstrate consent to the contact the claimant will fail to prove an essential element of this head of liability. That consent may be express or implied but in the sporting context it is usually implied from conduct. Participation in sport is generally considered to be a lawful justification for the giving of permission to be exposed to the risk of harm within the

---

40 Harrison v Vincent (supra, n.25).

41 [1965] 1 QB 232.

42 Wilson v Pringle [1987] QB 237.

boundaries of the rules and safeguards of the sport. The implied consent is usually taken to be consent to contact that can reasonably be expected to occur during the course of the sport although the extent of the consent given is a matter for the court to determine in light of all of the facts and circumstances of the case.[43]

The burden of proof in trespass remains on the claimant,[44] however where it is obvious that the contact in question was not consented to, the burden of proving a lawful excuse for the contact lies on the defendant. In most cases involving sporting contests the defendant will be able to demonstrate that implied consent to at least some contact was given and the real issue for the court will be whether the contact in question exceeded the extent of the consent given and thereby found a successful claim in trespass to the person.

Illustrations of liability

Liability has been demonstrated in circumstances[45] where assaults have occurred 'off the ball',[46] and where injury resulted as a result of a late tackle with two feet in an amateur football match.[47]

(3) LIABILITY IN CONTRACT

Although less common as a cause of action for damages for personal injury in the sporting context, there may be circumstances in which a claim in contract arises when considering careless activity on the sports field. Such circumstances might include those where a participant in an event agrees to abide by terms and conditions of entry, which may by express or implied terms require the participants to exercise at least reasonable care for their fellow competitors and spectators.[48] If the standard of care required by any such terms are no different to those

---

43 Blake v Galloway [2004] EWCA Civ 814 at para 21.

44 Fowler v Lanning [1959] 1 QB 426.

45 See also Grayson, *Sport & the Law*, 3rd edition, 1999 at 277.

46 R v Billinghurst [1978] Crim LR 553.

47 R v Barnes [2004] EWCA Crim 3246, although the criminal conviction overturned due to inadequate summing up to the jury by the trial judge.

imposed in negligence at common law then pleading the additional head of liability may confer no additional benefit but there may be circumstances in which the standard capable of being applied as a result of the contract are greater than those imposed in negligence or in which the contractual measure of damages differs from the tortious measure. It is therefore important for practitioners to consider whether on the facts of the particular case before them, there may be scope for such a contractual argument in addition to any perhaps more obvious complaint in negligence.[49]

48 It has been acknowledged by the courts that participation involves tacitly agreed understandings and conventions that are objectively ascertainable even in the absence of formal sporting rules – Blake v Galloway (supra, n.43).

49 And where the contract is with the organizer only, whether there is scope for the application of the Contracts (Rights of Third Parties) Act 1999.

CHAPTER TWO
LIABILITY OF THE PLAYER TO THE SPECTATOR

INTRODUCTION

In this section consideration is given to the circumstances in which a participant in a sporting event may be held liable to a spectator injured while attending an event. Such claims are commonly framed in negligence, with the operative allegation being that the participant failed to take reasonable care for the safety of the spectator rather than in trespass to the person.[1] While one may recall circumstances in which trespass might have been alleged had proceedings been brought,[2] the focus of this section is on claims advanced in negligence.

(1) LIABILITY IN NEGLIGENCE

In common with claims brought by participants against other participants, the cases in this area have generally been decided at the breach of duty stage, involving a consideration of the standard of care expected of the participant and whether on the facts that standard was met. The standard of care expected of a participant in such circumstances might be said to be generous to the participant - it was observed in Smoldon v Whitworth & Nolan,[3] when reviewing the case law dealing with injuries caused to spectators by players, that competitors are entitled to be all but oblivious to spectators while they are properly intent on winning the contest.

The leading case in this area remains Wooldridge v Sumner,[4] a case in which a photographer was injured by a competitor at an equestrian

1 The basic principles of demonstrating each head of liability are dealt with earlier in this chapter.

2 E.g. Eric Cantona kicking a Crystal Palace fan after being sent off in 1995 or Didier Drogba throwing a coin into a crowd of Burnley spectators in 2008.

3 [1997] ELR 249, per Lord Bingham LCJ at 256.

4 [1963] 2 QB 43.

event. The defendant galloped a horse around an arena at a speed such that a wide arc was necessary, the horse then went out of control and the photographer was struck when he attempted to protect a lady sitting on a bench adjacent to the arena. At first instance the plaintiff succeeded in negligence, the breach being the riding of the horse at too great a speed and the manner in which an attempt was made to bring the horse back into the arena. On appeal however the Court of Appeal held that the failures were 'mere errors of judgment' and did not amount to negligence in the circumstances. It was said that what the reasonable spectator would expect is as relevant as what the participant would expect.[5] Diplock LJ observed that:

> *"A reasonable spectator attending voluntarily to witness any game or competition knows and presumably desires that a reasonable participant will concentrate his attention upon winning, and if the game or competition is a fast-moving one, will have to exercise his judgment and attempt to exert his skill in what, in the analogous context of contributory negligence, is sometimes called "the agony of the moment." If the participant does so concentrate his attention and consequently does exercise his judgment and attempt to exert his skill in circumstances of this kind which are inherent in the game or competition in which he is taking part, the question whether any mistake he makes amounts to a breach of duty to take reasonable care must take account of those circumstances."*[6]

> *"The practical result of this analysis of the application of the common law of negligence to participant and spectator would, I think, be expressed by the common man in some such terms as these: 'A person attending a game or competition takes the risk of any damage caused to him by any act of a participant done in the course of and for the purposes of the game or competition notwithstanding that such act may involve an error of judgment or a lapse of skill,*

---

5 Per Diplock LJ at 67, citing Hall v Brooklands [1933] 1 KB 205, Scrutton LJ at 214.

6 At 67.

> *unless the participant's conduct is such as to evince a reckless disregard of the spectator's safety.' "*[7]

As will be seen below, in subsequent cases the test of *"reckless disregard"* has been adopted and applied.[8]

In Wilks v Cheltenham Homeguard Motor Cycle & Light Car Club,[9] a number of spectators were injured during the course of a motorcycle scrambling event, when they were lined up against a rope which marked out the spectator's enclosure. A motorcycle left the track at around 25-30mph and struck the spectators causing serious injury. It was held once more that in order to make out their claims the claimants had to demonstrate that the participant had shown a *"reckless disregard"* for their safety or that their injury was caused by an error of judgment that a reasonable competitor being a reasonable man of the sporting world would not have made, such that the error could not be reasonably regarded as excusable.

A distinction may be drawn between cases in which the error occurs in the course of the contest as opposed to the error of the participant occurring in the course of the pre-contest preparations, at which point there is a greater opportunity for the participant to reflect on their decisions. That is well illustrated by the case of Harrison v Vincent,[10] in which the defendant was held liable for injury to the passenger in the defendant's side car resulting from a failure to inspect and maintain the brake mechanism, but not as a result of an error during the course of the race when the defendant missed his gear once the brakes had failed. Similarly, the 'error of judgment in the heat of the moment' argument may not be available to a defendant who causes injury to a spectator not when actually competing. In Payne & Payne v Maple Leaf,[11] a parti-

---

7 At 68.

8 And as Beloff puts it, thus acknowledging the difference between a Carling colliding with a spectator and a Cantona kicking one (Beloff et. al., *Sports Law*, 2nd edition, 2012, p145, at 5.49).

9 [1971] 1 WLR 668.

10 [1982] RTR 8.

11 (1949) 1 DLR 369.

cipant was held liable to a spectator when the spectator was injured as a result of a fight between participants in an ice-hockey match, when not actually competing for the puck. Similarly, in Cleghorn v Oldham,[12] the defendant was held liable for an injury that resulted from a demonstration golf swing, where there was no 'heat of the moment' as such.

Cases on those distinct facts aside, the test of *"reckless disregard"* remains relevant when considering liability as between participants and spectators. The question might be posed however as to whether there is any good reason in principle why the test as between participants and spectators should be different from the test as it applies as between participants, with the question of whether the injury resulted from a mere error of judgment being taken into account when considering the appropriate standard of care and the participant's conduct. In Blake v Galloway,[13] Dyson LJ suggested that the test to be applied between participants in horseplay was analogous to that as had been applied in Wooldridge albeit, *"in a slightly expanded form"*.[14] Nevertheless, the position in Wooldridge and Wilks was confirmed as regards a participant's liability to a spectator by the Court of Appeal in in Smoldon,[15] albeit that the observations made in Smoldon were obiter.[16]

(2) LIABILITY IN NUISANCE

This section briefly considers the potential liability of the participant to the bystander or members of the public in the vicinity of the sporting venue. The bystander may or may not be a spectator but it is helpful to consider this potential head of liability at this point. It is also considered in Chapter 3 which deals with the liability of the owner or occupier of the sporting venue. While many of these cases have been brought against the owner or occupier of the venue in question the individual participant may equally be the subject of such a claim.

---

12 (1947) 43 TLR 465.

13 [2004] EWCA Civ 814.

14 At para 16.

15 Supra, n.3.

16 Per Lord Bingham LCJ at 256.

Liability in nuisance may be subdivided into private and public nuisance. A party may raise private nuisance as a cause of action in circumstances where there has been an interference with their reasonable use and enjoyment of their land. The claimant must have a proprietary or possessory interest in the land in question. In contrast, public nuisance is relied upon in circumstances where danger is caused to individuals located on a public highway. The difference is illustrated well by the cases in this area relating to damage caused by balls being struck beyond the boundaries of golf and cricket clubs. Where the injured party is located on the public highway then a claim may be brought in public nuisance, whereas where the claimant is located on their own adjoining land then private nuisance is the appropriate cause of action to consider.

Private nuisance is made out where the defendant has caused an interference with the claimant's reasonably enjoyment of his land, which has not otherwise been authorized.[17] It is to be determined by reference to the circumstances and the particular locality. In the sporting context that would necessarily involve a consideration of the frequency and consequences of the interference when it occurs. While coming to the nuisance is not a defence, it may be relevant as a feature of the locality which is to be taken into account or it may be a ground on which to refuse to order injunctive relief.

Illustrations of liability

Liability has been established in circumstances where a taxi-driver's windscreen was struck by a golf ball onto an adjoining highway,[18] where balls were hit out of the grounds of a golf club on regular basis and[19] in one case where 60,000 golf balls were hit over a fence each year.[20] Liability was not established in circumstances where cricket balls were hit out of the grounds of a cricket club but only rarely.[21] Liability has also been established in a number of cases involving noise nuisance asso-

17 Coventry & Ors v Lawrence & Ors [2014] UKSC 13, paras 3-4.

18 Castle v St Augustine's Links Ltd [1922] 38 TLR 615, public nuisance.

19 Miller v Jackson [1977] 1 QB 966, private nuisance.

20 Lamond v Glasgow Corporation (1968) SLT 291.

ciated with sporting activities although not resulting in personal injury.[22]

---

21 Bolton v Stone [1951] AC 850 and Potter v Carlisle & Cliftonville Golf Club [1939] NI 114.

22 Including Coventry & Ors v Lawrence & Ors [2014] UKSC 13, Watson v Croft Promo-sports Ltd [2009] 3 All ER 249 and East Dorset District Council v Eaglebeam Ltd & Ors [2006] EWHC 2378 (QB).

CHAPTER THREE
LIABILITY ARISING FROM THE CONDITION OF THE VENUE

INTRODUCTION

This chapter deals with the potential liability that may arise to participants, spectators, other visitors and non-visitors as a consequence of the condition of the place at which the event takes place, be it a stadium, court, track or pitch. Collectively they are referred to in this chapter as the sporting venue. This chapter also considers the circumstances in which liability might arise not as a result of any defective condition of the venue but rather as a result of the way in which the venue has been set up for the purposes of an event, so that while the venue may not be capable of being described as 'defective' as such, unnecessary risks of injury have been created or contributed to by the venue organisation.[1]

FORMS OF LIABILITY

An owner, occupier or organizer of the sporting venue in question may be held liable to the injured claimant as a result of the condition of the venue in negligence or breach of statutory duty, relying on the Occupiers' Liability Act 1957, the Occupiers' Liability Act 1984 and/or the Defective Premises Act 1972. Additionally, liability may also lie in contract in certain circumstances, e.g. where the spectator purchases a ticket to attend the venue to watch a sporting event. Each of these potential heads of liability are dealt with below.

Occupiers' Liability Act 1957

Section 2(1) of the Occupiers' Liability Act 1957 imposes on an occupier of premises a common duty of care owed to all visitors, to take such care as in all the circumstances of the case is reasonable to see that the visitor will be reasonably safe in using the premises for the purpose

---

1 See also Chapter 4 for discussion of the liability of the event organizer in such circumstances.

for which he or she has been invited or permitted by the occupier to be there.[2] The scope of the common duty of care owed under the 1957 Act depends in part on the purpose of the visit and the characteristics of the visitor. The occupier must expect a child to be less careful than an adult.[3] While warnings may be relevant and may in certain circumstances be sufficient to discharge the occupier's duty, generally speaking such warnings of hazards, without more, will not usually discharge the duty.[4] The independent contractor defence available at common law is preserved under the provisions of the 1957 Act,[5] as is *volenti non fit injuria*, to the extent that it may apply to sporting cases.[6]

The Act does not define the meaning of *"visitor"* or *"occupier"*, but in the context of participation of sporting events, the participant and the spectator who has purchased a ticket to the event will in all likelihood be considered visitors within the meaning of the 1957 Act. An *"occupier"* has been held to be any person who has sufficient control of the premises that they are able to make it safe.[7] As such there may be more than one occupier at any one time. Subject to the facts of the case then the owner of the venue and the organizer or promoter of the sporting event, if they are not one and the same, may both be considered to be occupiers for the purposes of considering a claim under the 1957 Act. As can be seen, the common duty of care imposed by section 2(2) is couched in similar terms to the general duty of care owed in negligence at common law. The application and effect of the common duty of care is perhaps best illustrated by reference to the reported cases, some of which are referred to below.

Occupiers' Liability Act 1984

The Occupiers' Liability 1984 deals with the liability of the occupier of the sporting venue to non-visitors, e.g. trespassers at the sporting venue.

2 Section 2(2) OLA 1957.

3 Section 2(3)(a) OLA 1957.

4 See section 2(4)(a) OLA 1957.

5 Section 2(4)(b) OLA 1957.

6 Section 2(5) OLA 1957 and for further commentary see Chapter 10.

7 Wheat v E. Lacon [1966] AC 552.

The circumstances in which the 1984 Act may be relevant are likely to be limited however one might foresee circumstances in which, for example, a spectator is present at a sporting venue without a ticket and as such has no permission to be there. In such circumstances the occupier of the venue would not be entitled to contend that no duty was owed to the non-visitor at all, rather section 1 of the 1984 Act would impose a duty of care on the occupier to the non-visitor in certain prescribed circumstances. An occupier for the purposes of the 1984 Act is the same as an occupier under the 1957 Act.[8] The duty owed to the non-visitor is to take reasonable care to ensure that the non-visitor does not suffer injury as a result of the danger.[9] However, the duty arises only in circumstances where the occupier is aware of has reasonable grounds for believing that the danger that caused the injury exists and he or she knows or has reasonable grounds to believe that the non-visitor is in the vicinity of the danger or that they may come into the vicinity of the danger, whether or not they have lawful authority to be there.[10] The likelihood of harm before the occupier is required to act has been said to be such as would impel a man of ordinary human feelings to take some steps to mitigate the risk of injury to the trespasser and depends on circumstances such as the permanent or intermittent nature of the danger, the severity of injury should injury occur, the extent to which children may be attracted to the danger, the expense involved in mitigating the risk and the occupier's resources.[11] The duty does not extend to protecting non-visitors from obvious risks arising from the natural condition of the premises and so no duty was owed by the owner of a swimming pool to take measures to protect non-visitors who might jump into the shallow end of their pool at night.[12]

---

8 Section 1(2)(a).

9 Section 1(4).

10 Section 1(3)(a) and (b).

11 British Railways Board v Herrington [1972] AC 844 at 941-942.

12 See James Evans v Kosmar Villa Holidays plc [2007] EWCA Civ 1003, [2008] 1 WLR 297, Luke William Ratcliff v (1) G R McConnell (2) E W Jones [1999] 1 WLR 670, CA and John Simon Donoghue v Folkestone Properties Ltd [2003] EWCA Civ 231, [2003] QB 1008, CA (diving into a harbor at night) and Tomlinson v Congleton Borough Council [2003] UKHL 47, [2004] 1 AC 46, [2003] 3 All ER 1122.

Defective Premises Act 1972

The Defective Premises Act 1972 may be relevant in circumstances where the danger at the premises may have resulted from a landlord's failure to maintain the premises contrary to the terms of any lease that may be in place. Section 4(1) of the 1972 Act imposes on a landlord a duty *"to all persons who might reasonably be expected to be affected by defects in the state of the premises ... to take such care as is reasonable in all the circumstances to see that they are reasonably safe from personal injury or from damage to their property caused by a relevant defect".* The duty is owed where the landlord knows or ought to have known of the defect,[13] thus where a landlord has a right to enter to inspect the premises but fails to do so with reasonable regularity and injury is caused as a result of a defect that would have been noted at an appropriate inspection, had one taken place, then the landlord may be held liable under section 4(1). If a sporting venue is let by a landlord to the organizer of an event, one can see how the 1972 Act may be relevant to the question of who is ultimately responsible should an injury result from the condition of the premises.

Liability in Contract

Liability may arise in contract in circumstances, for example, where the spectator purchases a ticket for an event from the organizer or promoter or where the participant contracts with the organizer or promoter to be involved in the contest. One case see that the terms of such contracts, whether express or implied, may include that in circumstances where the organizer is providing the venue or arranging for the provision of a venue that reasonable care has been taken to ensure that the venue is safe. Consideration might be given to this head of liability in the event that the measure of damages on the contractual basis is materially different to the tortious measure.[14]

---

13 Section 4(2).

14 Forward to the position that the claimant would have been in had there been no breach of contract versus back to the position the claimant would have been in had there been no negligent breach.

Negligence

By far the most common basis of claim in this area will be negligence at common law and the basic principles of liability of duty, breach and causation of loss and damage are considered elsewhere in more detail in this book.[15] In claims brought by visitors and non-visitors against owner and occupiers of premises it is commonplace for the claim to be pleaded in negligence alongside breach of the relevant particular statutory duty. Moreover, allegations of breach of duty in negligence may be supported with reference to statutory duties which do not carry with them a civil right of action for their breach, a number of which are referred to briefly below. Liability may arise in negligence as a result of the manner in which the sporting venue has been set up, without any suggestion of there being a defect in the state of the premises as such and so one can see that in cases where both negligence and breach of the Occupiers' Liability Act 1957 are alleged, negligence may have a much wider scope. Examples of such claims include those in which movable objects have been positioned as to pose a risk of injury to participants and spectators.[16]

Other sources of statutory duties

Other statutory duties which may or may not bring with them a civil right of action may be relevant in support of allegations of breach of duty in negligence and such legislation includes the Safety of Sports Grounds Act 1975, the Sporting Events (Control of Alcohol etc.) Act 1985, the Fire Safety and Safety of Places of Sport Act 1987, the Public Order Act 1986, the Football Spectators Act 1989, the Football (Offences) Act 1991, the Criminal Justice and Public Order Act 1994, the Football (Offences and Disorder) Act 1999 and the Sports Grounds Safety Authority Act 2011. In addition consideration may be given to regulations made under the Health & Safety at Work Act 1974 and in particular to the Workplace (Health, Safety & Welfare) Regulations

---

15 In particular, see Chapter 1.

16 E.g. as in Peter Corbett (by his wife and litigation friend Anita Corbett) v (1) Cumbria Kart Racing Club (2) Tracksport Challenge Ltd (3) RAC Motor Sports Association Ltd [2013] EWHC 1362 and Harrison v Vincent & Ors [1982] RTR 8, [1982] CLY 2159, CA, both referred to in more detail in Chapter 4.

1992 and the Management of Health & Safety at Work Regulations 1999, although from 1 October 2013 they no longer carry with them a right to bring an action for damages for their breach.[17]

Volenti non fit injuria

The defence of *volenti non fit injuria* is worth mentioning here as in a number of reported cases the defence has been advanced on the basis that the spectator,[18] visitor or participant has attended the sporting venue and has voluntarily accepted the risk associated with them having attended or having participated. A distinction might be drawn however between risks that materialize as a result of the sporting activity being undertaken at the venue as opposed to injury resulting from defects in the premises. In the latter, the defence can be expected to be given very short shrift, whereas it is may be more likely to amount to a reasonably arguable defence in the former circumstances.[19] A more detailed consideration is given to the issue of *volenti* in Chapter 10 however.

ILLUSTRATIVE CASES

Failure in the design or layout of the track or pitch

In Davis v Feasey[20] the claimant was a participant in a moto-cross event at the Corn Circle Scramble event near Hungerford. The track comprised hills, bends and jumps and the claimant was injured negotiating two raised earth banks, which were described as a 'double jump'. Double jumps were prohibited by the rules imposed by the sport's governing body on the basis that they presented an unacceptable danger. A claim was brought in negligence against the organizer of the event, who contended that the track feature was not a 'double jump' but rather was a 'roll-over', i.e. an obstacle that a rider negotiates by riding over, which

17 An amendment to section 49 of the Health & Safety at Work Act 1974, introduced by section 69 of the Enterprise and Regulatory Reform Act 2013 – see Chapter 6 for further discussion of the effect of this change.

18 E.g. **Hall v Brooklands Auto Racing Club [1933] 1 KB 205.**

19 As in Wooldridge v Sumner [1963] 2 QB 43.

20 Richard Davis v Pat Feasey & Anor, LTL 14/5/1998, CA.

was permitted by the rules and as the danger complained of was simply one that was normal and inherent within the sport. At first instance it was found that the feature was a double jump and concluded that the track layout was unduly dangerous, even in the context of a dangerous sport. It was said that simple steps could have been take to reduce the risk from the hazard. However the defendant's case was not helped by the fact that they opted to call no evidence.

Similarly, in Glenie v Slack & Barclay,[21] the claim arose out of an accident that occurred at a motor racing track at the Matchams Leisure Park in Hampshire. The claimant was riding a motorcycle with a passenger in the attached sidecar around the track in a practice session prior to a race scheduled to take place in the evening. The motorcycle came into contact with a fence that ran around the inside of the track and a collision followed resulting in the claimant being seriously injured and rendered paraplegic, while the passenger in the sidecar was killed. Proceedings were brought against the owner of the track and the organizer of the event, relying on negligence at common law and the Occupiers' Liability Act 1957. The claimant contended that the track was unsafe as there was no unobstructed central run-off area, an unusual feature. The fence with which the claimant collided was positioned there to separate the track from the immediately adjacent stock car track. The claimant also contended that the surface of the track was unsafe. The first defendant contended that the claimant was not a lawful visitor to the track, that in any event it had a defence of *volenti non fit injuria* as regards the risk of collision with the inner fence and that the sport was inherently dangerous and any duty of care had to be limited by reference to that fact. The second defendant, organizer, denied that he was an occupier. It was said that the accident had occurred before the race meeting had started and after the claimant had been denied permission to race. It was held that the track was inherently unsafe as a result of the inner fence. Expert evidence confirmed that sidecars required a safe run off area on the infield as a result of their design and of their direction of travel should control be lost. The fence was held to have posed a clearly foreseeable risk of injury such that the

21 Glenie v Slack & Barclay, 11/12/1998, LTL 1/1/1999 (first instance), 19/4/2000, [2000] All ER (D) 592, CA.

racetrack was not suitable for sidecar racing. The court found that both defendants were occupiers within the 1957 Act and that the claimant was a lawful visitor. A single simple notice which did not suggest that the effect of any failure to sign on to race would be that the racer would not be there as a visitor was not sufficient to result in the claimant being categorized as trespasser. The owner and occupier had taken advice on the design of the track from someone within the first defendant's employment but it was also held that the danger should have been obvious to the second defendant who was an experienced racer. It was found that with an adequate run off area the claimant probably would have done more to recover. The defence of *volenti* was not made out as no one pointed out the danger to the claimant and he did not appreciate it, but if he had appreciated he had not consented to the consequences of it. The court found contributory negligence on the part of the claimant of 50% as he was aware of the inexperience of his passenger, of their lack of brakes and of their bias towards the infield and as he could have done more to have avoided the collision. The first defendant owner was found two thirds responsible for the balance and the organizer one third. The appeal of the first defendant (on the basis that the sport was inherently dangerous and as occupier he had handed the track over to the second defendant and as such owed the claimant no duty) and the cross-appeal of the claimant (against the extent of the finding of contributory negligence) were both dismissed on the basis that the trial judge's conclusions were correct.

Likewise, in Wattleworth v Goodwood Road Racing Co Ltd,[22] the deceased died when he crashed into a tyre-faced earth bank during an amateur track day at the Goodwood circuit, owned and operated by the first defendant. Proceedings were brought against Goodwood, the national governing body and licensing authority, the RAC Motor Sports Association and the international governing body the Federation De Internationale Automobile. Claims were brought in negligence and under the Occupiers' Liability Act 1957. The death was held to have resulted from poor track design and in particular the selection of the tyre structure to front he earth bank, as the tyres pocketed rather than

22 Wattleworth v Goodwood Road Racing Co Ltd [2004] EWHC 140 (QB), [2004] PIQR P25, [2004] All ER (D) 51 (Feb) (see also Chapter 6 in respect of the liability of the governing body).

causing the claimant to slide along the front of the tyres once a collision had occurred. The first and second defendants owed the claimant a duty of care, the second defendant because it had assumed responsibility for safety inspections at the circuit. However, breach was not established on the evidence before the court. The first defendant had reasonably relied on the expertise of the second defendant and the design and construction of the safety measure was held to have met a reasonable standard of safety.[23]

In Simms v Leigh Rugby Football Club Ltd,[24] a rugby player brought proceedings having been injured during the course of a rugby match played on a pitch belonging to and occupied by the defendant. His injury arose as a result of the presence of a concrete wall running at a distance of approximately 7' 3" from touchline on one side of the pitch. had gathered the ball and run with it to the try-line. At the moment of reaching the try-line at a point where it formed a corner with the touchline he was tackled by one or two opposing players and thrown towards the concrete wall. As a result his leg was broken. The evidence was not clear whether plaintiff's leg came into contact with the concrete wall and the claim was dismissed on that basis, with it being concluded that a broken leg associated with an ordinary tackle being an inherent risk of the game, but also as the location of the wall did not infringe the byelaws of Rugby League, which provided that there should be a clear area measuring at least 7 feet and which had been laid down by the sport's governing body.[25] A duty was owed under the 1957 Act but the risk was foreseeable but so improbable that it did not require measures to be taken to prevent it. The claimant was also held to have willingly accepted the risks of playing on the pitch, relying on s.2(5) of the 1957 Act.

---

23 Similarly, the layout of the circuit was found to have been safe in Stratton v (1) Hughes (Executrix of the Estate of Edward John Hughes) (2) Cumberland Sporting Car Club Limited (3) RAC Motor Sports Association Ltd, unreported, February 28, 1997, QBD but unsafe in Latchford v Spedeworth International Ltd (1984) 134 NLJ, Times, October 11, 1983, QBD – see Chapter 4.

24 [1969] 2 All ER 923.

25 Further discussion of the governing body's potential liability can be found in Chapter 6.

Failures to inspect the circuit and to install necessary safety measures

In Fenton v Thruxton (BARC) Ltd,[26] the claimant attended the first defendant's racetrack as a spectator in order to watch the British Superbike Championship. The second defendant governing body had inspected and approved the circuit as safe prior to the race. At the time of his injury the claimant was sitting in a designated spectator area close to a right-hand bend in the circuit. A motorcycle left the track at the corner during the race and crashed into the area where the claimant was sitting, causing him injury. At trial the claimant contended that the seating area was inadequately protected and that the first defendant, as tenant and occupier, was in breach of its common law duty to him or in breach of its duty to him under the Occupiers' Liability Act 1957. The first defendant admitted that it owed a duty to the claimant to ensure that the circuit was reasonably safe, but denied breach of duty on the basis that it had reasonably relied on independent advice given to it by the second defendant. The claimant contended that the second defendant owed a duty to him and that there was a breach of duty in that its track inspector had failed to require the first defendant to install a debris fence. It was held that the first defendant was liable as an occupier of a racetrack to which paying spectators were admitted notwithstanding its reliance on the second defendant's inspector. It was considered that it was under an obligation to satisfy itself that reasonable steps had been taken to ensure the safety of spectators and the first defendant had failed to satisfy itself that the inspections were properly carried out. The second defendant was also held to owe the claimant a duty of care. The court then determined that the test to be applied when considering the issue of breach of that duty was whether the second defendant's expert had directed his mind to the question of comparative risks and benefits and reached a defensible conclusion on the matter.[27] It was found that the pre-accident track inspection had not involved identifying and evaluating the comparative risks and that

26 Michael Derek Fenton v (1) Thruxton (BARC) Ltd (2) Motorcycle Circuit Racing Control Board Ltd, December 12, 2008, Basingstoke CC and see also [2009] EWCA Civ 652, LTL 14/5/2009 (application for permission to appeal).

27 Thus effectively applying the Bolam test (see Bolam v Friern Hospital Management Committee [1957] 1 WLR 582 and Bolitho v City & Hackney Health Authority [1998] AC 232).

the inspector had failed to consider the safety requirements of competitors, officials and spectators, with each class of individual having different characteristics and requirements. It was held that whilst motor racing was dangerous and accidents happen, reasonable precautions are required to reduce the risk of harm and there was no evidence that the pre-accident track inspections had been directed to spectators' safety.

In the older case of Hall v Brooklands,[28] a spectator brought proceedings after being seriously injured when two cars collided near to a spectator railing with the result that one of the cars travelled through the railing and into the spectators' stand. At first instance a jury found that there had been a failure to take reasonable precautions. However, on appeal the Court of Appeal held that it was the duty of the owner/organizer to see that the course was as free from danger as reasonable care and skill could make it, but that it was not the insurer against accidents that no reasonable diligence would have foreseen or against inherent dangers in the sport that the reasonable spectator should have foreseen and of which he takes the risk. It was determined that there was no evidence that the defendant had failed to take reasonable care for the safety of the spectators.

A perhaps surprising decision was reached in Murray v Haringey Arena Ltd,[29] in which a 6-year-old boy was struck over the left eye by a hockey puck at an ice hockey match, resulting in the impairment of his vision. The claimant was seated in the spectator's enclosure in the defendant's arena. In proceedings brought in negligence the court held that there was no implied obligation on the defendant under the contract made between the parties to protect him from such dangers as might be incidental to the game, which any spectator could reasonably foresee and of which he took the risk.[30] The decision is perhaps explicable if one considers when it was decided and the fact that the rejection of the defence of *volenti non fit injuria* came in subsequent cases. The outcome of this

---

28 Hall v. Brooklands Auto Racing Club [1933] 1 KB 205.

29 [1951] 2 KB 529.

30 Applying the decision in Hall v. Brooklands Auto Racing Club [1933] 1 KB 205.

case might suggest that liability is less likely to be established where the injury results notwithstanding compliance with the rules of the sport,[31] that being what spectators pay to see, but the position is different in circumstances where the premises are defective, e.g. in the case of a collapsing grandstand.[32]

Similarly, in Wilks v Cheltenham Home Guard Motorcycle & Light Car Club,[33] the claimants were spectators at a motorcycle scramble meeting and were positioned in the spectators' enclosure, which was alongside a straight stretch of the course around 150-200 yards long. They were lined up against a rope beyond which there was a 10-foot wide 'no mans land' and then a further 'wrecking rope' running along the side of the track. During the course of the event the second defendant motorcycle rider veered to one side, crossed the ropes and landed with his cycle amongst the spectators, injuring the claimants. The course had been approved by officials of the Auto-Cycle Union and the trial judge found that the organizers of the scramble not responsible for the injury. The second defendant rider was found liable for negligence in the manner of his riding, which decision was overturned on appeal on the basis that in the context of the nature of the sport there could be no inference drawn of negligence from the mere fact of the accident and *res ipsa loquitur* was not a principle that could assist the claimant on the facts of the case.

In Wilkins v Smith,[34] a number of girls were being coached in discus throwing at an athletics club. The claimant was one of the girls and was standing well back behind a cage of netting from which another girl was throwing the discus. When thrown the discus hit a taut guy rope at the mouth of the cage, ricocheted and struck the claimant. She brought proceedings for damages in negligence against the owners of the club. The court found that the defendant owed a duty to those within the

---

31 See the observation to that effect in Kevan et al., Sports Personal Injury: Law & Practice (2002) at 5.06.

32 As in Francis v Cockrell (1870) LR 5 QB 501.

33 [1971] 3 All ER 369.

34 (1976) 73 Law Soc Gaz 938.

range of the discus, to protect them from deflections from the guy ropes, however the claimant was in such an area that no such duty was owed and on the facts of the case the discus had taken an extraordinary course.

The provision and position of safety measures on the course were also considered in Hide v Steeplechase Co (Cheltenham) Ltd.[35] The claimant was a jockey participating in a horse race. On clearing the first hurdle, his horse stumbled and fell, causing him to fall, hit the ground and to travel into a post holding up the rail running around the outside of the track. The claimant brought proceedings under the Provision and Use of Work Equipment Regulations 1998 contending that the hurdle was placed too close to the perimeter rail, which was insufficiently padded. At first instance the judge imported a test of *"reasonable foreseeability"* into Regulation 4, found that the accident had occurred in a very unusual way, that the defendant had complied with the requirements laid down by the British Horseracing Authority, and that both the hurdle and rail were suitable. The Court of Appeal overturned the decision on the basis that while the Regulation defined *"suitable"* as being *"suitable in any respect which it is reasonably foreseeable will affect the health or safety of any person"*, there was no such concept in the Directive that the Regulations were intended to implement. The only basis on which a defendant could avoid liability under the Directive was if the accident resulted from an occurrence due to unforeseeable circumstances beyond its control or due to exceptional events, the consequences of which were unavoidable despite the exercise of all due care. The words "reasonably foreseeable" therefore fell to be construed in a way which was consistent with the limited concept of foreseeability envisaged by the Directive. It was therefore for the defendant to prove that the accident was attributable to either category of occurrence envisaged in the Directive. It followed that the judge in the instant case was incorrect to import into Regulation 4 the classic common law phrase of reasonable foreseeability and to dismiss the claim. This case should now be considered in light of the amendment to section 49 of the Health & Safety at Work Act 1974 introduced by

35 [2014] 1 All ER 405, [2013] PIQR P22.

section 69 of the Enterprise and Regulatory Reform Act 2013 however.[36]

Unsafe installations / equipment on the pitch

In Hall v Holker Estate Co Ltd,[37] the claimant was injured playing football with his father at a caravan park owned and occupied by the defendant. The defendant had erected a portable tubular goal frame on a grassed area for visitors to use but had not secured the goal frame to the ground adequately. The claimant tripped when he went to retrieve the ball, the frame fell forwards and the cross bar struck him on the head. The court heard evidence that included that the defendant was aware that visitors and children had removed pegs from the goal posts on occasions in the past. At trial the claim was dismissed on the basis that the accident was unusual and after inferring that the situation as it appeared at the time of the accident had been so only for a short period of time. It was found that there had not been daily inspections of the goal net, but no finding as to what an appropriate inspection interval was. The Court of Appeal upheld the claimant's appeal on the basis that once the judge had found that the accident had resulted from a want of safety due to the absence of pegs and that there was a known risk against which counter measures were called for, a duty arose to devise and implement a suitable system of inspection.[38] It was held that there was no evidence to support the conclusion that the goal had not been in an unsafe state for long and appeal was allowed.

Dangerous items/debris left on the pitch

In Sutton v Syston Rugby Football Club Ltd,[39] the claimant was injured in a rugby training session organized by the defendant when he fell on a broken cricket boundary marker that had been left on the field. The claimant contended that there was a duty on the defendant to

36 See further discussion in Chapter 6.

37 Hall v Holker Estate Co Ltd [2008] EWCA Civ 1422, LTL 17/12/2008, [2008] NPC 143.

38 Applying Ward v Tesco Stores Ltd [1976] 1 WLR 810.

39 Sutton v Syston Rugby Football Club Ltd [2011] EWCA Civ 1182, [2011] All ER (D) 182 (Oct).

undertake an inspection of the pitch before the training session began. The defendant admitted the existence of the duty to undertake a general inspection of the pitch, but contended that such an inspection would only have revealed obvious risks and would not have identified the broken cricket boundary marker as it did not protrude above the surface of the grass. The claimant succeeded at first instance on the basis that an inspection should have been performed at reasonable walking pace, that more care was required to inspect the ends of the pitch where players could be expected to touch down and that such an inspection would have identified the hazard. The Court of Appeal confirmed that there was a duty to inspect the pitch and while the injury occurred during a practice session, reference was made to the RFU risk assessment guidelines, which recommended checks for foreign objects prior to matches. It was said to be over-complicated to expect different standards of care in respects of different parts of the pitch and that it was important that standards were not set which were too difficult for ordinary coaches and organizers to meet. An observation was also made that rugby was a desirable activity within the meaning of s.1 of the Compensation Act 2006. The appeal was allowed and the claim dismissed on the basis that a reasonable system of inspection would not have identified the hazard.

The observation that it was unnecessarily complicated to require different standards of care in respect of different parts of the pitch seems surprising. One might have expected the Court of Appeal to take the view that a single standard of 'reasonable care' applied to the whole pitch, but that in relation to areas where it was known that players would land on the ground, such reasonable care required a greater level of scrutiny. In the context of claims brought against Highway Authorities for negligent inspections of the highway performed in order to discharge the duty owed under section 41 of Highways Act 1980 to maintain highways maintain able at the public expense, inspectors are not permitted to ignore areas located under parked vehicles and the level of scrutiny expected varies depending on the known footfall.

Dangerous condition and failure to maintain

In Brown v Lewis,[40] the claimant was injured as a result of a collapsing stand at Blackburn Rovers Football Club. The club was found liable in respect of the claimant's injury, which resulted from them engaging an incompetent contractor to repair defects.[41]

Liability for defective venue enabling an assault

In the perhaps surprising case of Cunningham v Reading Football Club,[42] a claim was brought by a number of police officers who were injured by pieces of broken concrete broken off from a defective structure at a football ground and which were then thrown by hooligans at a football match. It was held that the club had failed to maintain the structure and that it knew or ought to have known of the risk that visiting hooligans might use pieces of concrete as missiles. As such it was held liable to the claimants under section 2 of the Occupiers' Liability Act 1957.

Liability for negligent setting up of the venue

In Green v Sunset & Vine Productions Ltd,[43] an experienced racing driver was injured when the racing car he was driving at the Goodwood racing circuit clipped a kerb and hit a tyre wall. The first defendant had a contract with Goodwood, the promoter, to produce outside broadcasts for the meeting. The second defendant was the event organizer. The claimant's case was that the accident had resulted from the wheels of his car hitting a "kerb cam" which had been placed at a dangerous point on the track. At first instance the court found that the claimant's accident was caused by his own error of judgment and that he had cornered too fast for the line he had taken, crossed the kerb and

40 (1896) 12 TLR 455.

41 See also Francis v Cockrell (1870) LR 5 QB 501.

42 Cunningham v Reading Football Club Limited [1992] PIQR P141, (1991) The Times, 22 March.

43 Malcolm William Green v (1) Sunset & Vine Productions Ltd (2) British Automobile Racing Club Ltd [2010] EWCA Civ 1441, [2010] 2 All ER (D) 193.

unsettled the car. It was held that insofar as there may have been negligence in the placing of the kerb cam, it had not been causative. The claimant's appeal failed on the grounds that the judge was entitled reach the findings that he had and that the claimant had not established that the camera or cable attached to it had been installed in a negligent manner.

In Harrison v Vincent,[44] the organizers of a motorcycle and sidecar racing event had parked a recovery vehicle 30-40 metres from the course on a slip road that was intended to provide an escape route for vehicles should they leave the circuit at a particular bend. The recovery vehicle projected two feet into the road. The rear brake failed as the motorcycle and sidecar combination took the bend, they left the track and struck the recovery vehicle. The claimant, who was the passenger in the sidecar suffered injury and brought successful proceedings against the motorcycle rider and the organizer in negligence. The organizer was held to have been required to consider the foreseeable risk of vehicles needing to use escape routes and to keep them clear. The rider was held liable for the failure of the brakes on the motorcycle, but not for his response once faced with the emergency.

---

44 Peter Corbett (by his wife and litigation friend Anita Corbett) v (1) Cumbria Kart Racing Club (2) Tracksport Challenge Ltd (3) RAC Motor Sports Association Ltd [2013] EWHC 1362.

CHAPTER FOUR
LIABILITY OF THE PROMOTER & ORGANISER

INTRODUCTION

In this chapter we discuss the way in which liability on the part of a promoter or organizer of a sporting event might arise, with reference to a number of illustrative cases. The liability of the organizer and promoter for the state of premises or as a result of their status as occupier under the Occupiers' Liability legislation is considered elsewhere in this book.[1] A detailed discussion of vicarious liability is dealt with elsewhere in this book.[2]

THE ORGANISER AND PROMOTER

As the party responsible for the bringing together of the venue, the officials, the participants and the spectators to a sporting event and for the planning and provision of all of those features necessary to ensure that a challenging, entertaining yet safe competition has been arranged, one can see that the organiser or promoter may be the first port of call should things not go as planned with the result that individuals suffer injury. In the sphere of boxing that may be the promoter. It is notable that in Watson v British Boxing Board of Control,[3] while the governing body laid down minimum safety requirements to be implemented by the promoter, it was noted by Lord Phillips that[4]:

> *"It seems to me that, but for the intervention of the board, the promoter would probably owe a common law duty to the boxer to make reasonable provision for the immediate treatment of his injuries."*

---

1 See Chapter 3.

2 See Chapter 10.

3 Watson v British Boxing Board of Control Ltd [2001] QB 1134, CA.

4 At p1160, paragraph 78.

While not usually so in the case of boxing, in other sports the organizer is often also the owner or occupier of the sporting venue and as such the organizer's responsibilities arising from them acting in that capacity should be considered, under the Occupiers' Liability Act 1957 and 1984 and the Defective Premises Act 1972 for example.[5]

Away from the issue of the organiser's liability as owner or occupier of the venue however, the starting point when considering the responsibilities of the organizer is the need for them to have performed a suitable and sufficient risk assessment in respect of the activity being performed. Such a risk assessment would usually inform the organizer as to the measures reasonably required to secure the safety of the participants and spectators, as to who should be consulted for advice, as to who should be employed or engaged and as to what training they should have, among other things. Generally speaking, these are the most common areas where breach is alleged as against such defendants.

Thus, in Corbett v Cumbria Kart Racing Club,[6] the claimant brought proceedings for damages against a motor racing club and the organizer of a moped racing event, when his motorcycle and sidecar outfit left the track at a bend during the course of a race, continued across grass and tarmac before striking a tyre barrier and an ambulance that had been parked being it. It was found that the cause of the claimant's serious head injury was the collision with the ambulance. The court held that it was foreseeable that motorcycles might come off the track at the bend in question, that that was the sort of thing that any reasonably prudent organizer of a race meeting would have in mind when considering the safety of the track and competitors, that there was no sensible reason for the positioning of the ambulance and that is posed a foreseeable risk of injury. There were no adequate risk assessments in place and the organizer was found liable for the claimant's injury. The organizer

5 See chapter 3 which includes reference to Andrew Guy Glenie v (1) Reginald Slack & (2) Ian Barclay (unreported) April 19, 2000, CA, where the organiser's liability to the claimant arose principally as a result of its control over the race track in question and the application of the Occupiers' Liability Act 1957.

6 Peter Corbett (by his wife and litigation friend Anita Corbett) v (1) Cumbria Kart Racing Club (2) Tracksport Challenge Ltd (3) RAC Motor Sports Association Ltd [2013] EWHC 1362.

sought to rely on inspections undertaken over 4 years prior to the accident by the MSA, however proceedings against the governing body were discontinued prior to trial.

Similarly, in Harrison v Vincent & Ors,[7] the claimant suffered injury during the course of a motor racing event arranged by the defendant race organizer, the Scarborough District Motor Club. The claimant was a passenger in a sidecar being driven by the first defendant. During the course of the race the rear brake on the motorcycle and sidecar failed and the first defendant was forced to leave the track. The motorcycle and sidecar went on to strike a recovery vehicle parked on a slip road 30-40 metres from the track but which protruded 2 feet into the slip road. The defendant organizer was held liable for the location of the recovery vehicle as it was positioned contrary to an international code of practice standing order which require slip roads to be kept clear for at least 100 metres. The Court of Appeal confirmed that the race organiser was required to consider and take steps to guard against risks that might arise in such circumstances, which included keeping escape routes clear.

In Latchford v Spedeworth International Ltd,[8] the claimant was injured when driving in a hot rod motor race, when his car struck a tyre guard which had been displaced by another car from a concrete flower bed that it had been shielding. The organizer was held liable on the basis that it was responsible for the safety of the tyre guard. The defendant's defence of *volenti* failed as the defendant had not demonstrated that the claimant had full appreciation of the nature and extent of the risks.

An organiser successfully defended a claim brought against it in Stratton v Hughes.[9] In that case, the claimant was injured during the course of a national rally championship event. The claimant brought a claim for damages against his deceased co-driver and the rally organisers criticizing the driving of his co-driver, the illegal installation of a bias brake

7 [1982] RTR 8, [1982] CLY 2159, CA.

8 (1984) 134 NLJ 36, Times, October 11, 1983, QBD.

9 Stratton v (1) Hughes (Executrix of the Estate of Edward John Hughes) (2) Cumberland Sporting Car Club Limited (3) RAC Motor Sports Association Ltd, unreported, February 28, 1997, Steele J., QBD.

valve in the Toyota involved and the layout of the course, as against the second and third defendants. The organizer was held to have owed a duty of care to the claimant but the layout of the course was found not to have been unsafe.

In Craven v Riches,[10] the claimant was injured during a weekend motorcycle event organized by the first defendant at the second defendant's track at Knockhill. The claimant was riding his own 900cc motorcycle after not having ridden it for a year. The event was described as an opportunity for motorcyclists to have ride around the track rather than being a race. The participants were divided into three groups according to their speed and the claimant was entered into the fast group. He completed a number of laps of the track, increasing his speed on each lap as he gained confidence. On his final lap the claimant reached 125mph, came over the brow of a hill, saw other riders to his left travelling slowly and approaching a corner. He braked, lost control and sustained serious injuries when his bike left the track. The claimant brought proceedings against the organizer and track owner in negligence and for breach of duty under the Occupiers Liability (Scotland) Act 1960, contending that motorcycles travelling in the slow group should not have been on the track at the same time as the fast group. The claim was dismissed at first instance, the judge finding that although having riders from the three groups on the track at the same time was not the safest way to arrange the proceedings, there was no breach of duty and the congestion that resulted was not a cause of the accident. The decision was overturned on appeal, with the appeal court concluding that the organizer's duty extended to preventing obstructions to faster riders by slower riders, to ensuring that faster riders did not come across slow riders on the track unexpectedly, that the claimant's speed was predictable and the approach to slow riders at that predictable speed created the risk of an accident, an obvious way to avoid that risk was to not let slow riders on the track at the same time as fast riders, but the critical issue was not the presence of a disparity of speeds, but the magnitude of that disparity. It was held that it was one thing for a fast rider to be aware of other riders going slower, but it was something different to expect him to expect riders travelling at danger-

10 [2001] EWCA Civ 375, [2002] PIQR P320.

ously slow speeds. A finding of contributory negligence of two-thirds was made however given that the claimant was inexperienced with the machine he was riding and particularly at high speeds.

Finally, in Paul Stanley v Bryn Close t/a Amthorpe Moto Parc,[11] the first and second claimants had been racing on a motor track operated by the defendant. Their motorcycles collided at the twelfth jump when a marshal failed to display a yellow flag, indicating that caution was required as an obstruction was ahead. The first claimant had stalled and was stationary as the second claimant approached. It was held that despite the provision of training, the defendant had failed to ensure that the marshaling at the course was adequate and was vicariously liable for the marshal's conduct.

Thus, the sports lawyer considering the liability the organizer and promoter should consider issues relevant to the state of the sporting venue, for which the organizer or promoter may be liable, but also for things done on the premises, which arise out of the organiser's responsibility to undertake an appropriate risk assessment and to put in place such measures as a sufficient risk assessment requires so as to ameliorate or remove the risks identified, insofar as that may be possible in the circumstances.

---

11 [2009] EWHC 2849 (QB), LTL 15/2/2010.

CHAPTER FIVE
LIABILITY OF THE OFFICIAL & THE SPORTS COACH

INTRODUCTION

This chapter deals with the potential liability of the sporting official, i.e. the referee or umpire, in respect of injury sustained on the field by participants and players and with claims brought against the sports coach or supervisor. Such claims are usually brought in negligence at common law, the basic principles of which are considered in Chapter 1, which deals with the liability of the player.

(1) LIABILITY OF THE REFEREE AND UMPIRE

A referee or umpire owes a duty of care to players to enforce the rules of the sport in order to minimize the risks of injury that may be inherent in the game.[1] The majority of cases dealing with the liability of the official turn on the question of breach of duty, and determinations as to the appropriate standard of care to be applied and whether on the facts the referee's or umpire's conduct failed to meet that standard. In cases involving child participants, while the duty owed may be the same as in any other case, the fact that the participants are children and may be inexperienced in the activity may well feed in to the question of the standard of care expected of the referee or umpire.

The leading case in this area remains Smoldon v Whitworth & Nolan.[2] The plaintiff was 17 years old and the hooker and captain of the Sutton Coldfield colts rugby team. He suffered a serious injury to his neck when a scrum collapsed. At first instance the trial judge dismissed the claim brought against the opposing player but found the referee liable

---

1 See Bartlett v English Cricket Board Association of Cricket Officials, 27 Aug 2015, reported Lawtel, 3 Sep 2015, unreported elsewhere (cricket umpire), Smoldon v Whitworth & Nolan [1997] PIQR P133 and [1997] ELR 249, CA, Vowles v Evans & Welsh Rugby Union Ltd [2003] EWCA Civ 318 and see also Allport v Wilbraham [2004] EWCA Civ 1668 (rugby referee).

2 Smoldon v Whitworth & Nolan [1997] PIQR P133 and [1997] ELR 249, CA.

for failing to control the pack. The Court of Appeal dismissed the referee's appeal. Lord Bingham LCJ delivering the judgment of the court observed that there had been no previous reported case in which a rugby player had successfully sued a referee in negligence. It was held that the trial judge had correctly applied the standard of care as suggested in Condon v Basi,[3] i.e. that the duty on the referee was to take such care as was appropriate in all the circumstances and that the test was not one of whether the referee had evinced a 'reckless disregard' for the safety of the players.[4]

As to the standard of care expected the Court of Appeal held that, *"The level of care required is that which is appropriate in all the circumstances and the circumstances are of crucial importance. Full account must be taken of the factual context in which a referee exercises his functions and he could not properly be held liable for errors of judgment, oversights or lapses of which any referee might be guilty in the context of a fast-moving and vigorous contest. The threshold of liability is a high one. It will not easily be crossed"*.[5]

The case law pertaining to the liability of participants to spectators was distinguished on the basis that the position of a referee vis-à-vis a player is not the same as the position of a participant vis-à-vis a spectator as the referee has a positive responsibility to safeguard the players. It was said that, *"although the legal duty is the same in the two cases, the practical content of the duty differs according to the quite different circumstances"*.[6] The defendant argued that the standard of care was informed by the grade of the referee in question, while the plaintiff contended that the standard should be assessed by reference to the function the referee was performing and not his grade. While it made no difference to the outcome on the facts, the court preferred the plaintiff's formulation.[7] It was also held that it was not necessary for the plaintiff to have to prove

3 [1985] 1 WLR 866.

4 The formulation in the spectator cases of Wooldridge v Sumner [1963] 2 QB 43 and Wilks v Cheltenham Homeguard Motor Cycle & Light Car Club [1971] 1 WLR 668.

5 [1997] ELR 249 at 256.

6 Ibid at 256.

that there was a high level of probability that the scrum would collapse, but rather it was sufficient for him to demonstrate that serious injury was a probable consequence should there be a failure to prevent the scrum collapsing. A defence of *volenti non fit injuria* was also rejected on the basis that only the usual risks of the sport had been the subject of the plaintiff's consent and he had not consented to risks associated with a breach of duty on the part of the official whose duty it was to ensure, so far as possible, that the rules were observed.

In the subsequent case of Vowles v Evans & Welsh Rugby Union Ltd,[8] once more a referee of an amateur rugby match was held liable for injuries that resulted from the collapse of a scrum. During the course of play a prop suffered a dislocated shoulder and was replaced by a flanker who then played as a prop. The defendant referee had given the team the option of playing with a replacement or of continuing with non-contested scrums. It was found that the defendant had failed to enquire whether the flanker had any previous experience of playing as prop contrary to law 3(12) of the game and that he should not have offered the captain of that team the option of continuing with anything other than non-contested scrums. It was determined at trial that the claimant was injured as a result of the flanker's inexperience. An argument was advanced at trial that in fact no duty at all was owed to players by the referee (relying on the Australian case of Agar v Hyde,[9] in which the governing body the International Rugby Board was held to owe no duty to players in rugby matches) however the Court of Appeal upheld the trial judge's conclusion that it was fair, just and reasonable for a duty of care to be owed by the referee and distinguished Agar v Hyde. It was relevant that rugby was an inherently dangerous sport but it was also significant that the role of the referee was to enforce the rules some of which were designed to minimize the risk of injury. It was considered that where a referee undertakes that role it is reasonable for players to expect the referee to exercise reasonable care in doing so. It was also acknowledged once more however that the threshold for liability is high

---

7 Ibid at 257. See also Chapter 1 for a discussion of the relevance of the skill of the defendant in setting the appropriate standard of care.

8 Vowles v Evans & Welsh Rugby Union Ltd [2003] EWCA Civ 318.

9 [2001] HCA 41.

although the standard of care owed depended on all of the circumstances of the case. On the facts of the case the first defendant was held liable for the claimant's injuries and the second defendant vicariously liable for the first defendant's breach.[10]

More recently, in Bartlett v English Cricket Board Association of Cricket Officials,[11] it was held that although a referee in a fast-moving game might not be in a position to avoid errors of judgment, the position might be different when there is the opportunity to consider the decision or conduct that is the subject of criticism. The claimant was the captain of a cricket team who had expressed a view to officials that a match should be postponed as a result of previous heavy rainfall, which it was said made the pitch unsafe. The officials inspection the pitch and determined that it was safe. The claimant was injured during the course of the game when he performed a sliding stop. It was determined that although the threshold for liability was high, the threshold was lower on the particular facts of this case as the defendant had the opportunity to reflect on the decision that was made and as it was not one made in the heat of the moment or in the course of a fast-moving or vigorous contest. The claimant's claim failed however as the court found as a fact that the pitch was not so unsafe as to render it dangerous such that the decision of the match officials was negligent.

The state of the law in relation to the liability of a referee to the player remains as originally stated in Smoldon and applied in Vowles. Central to the imposition of the duty of care is the function of the referee or umpire which includes the application and enforcement of rules designed to protect participants from injury. The standard of care is that which is appropriate taking account of all of the circumstances of the case, which will include whether the responsibilities of the referee or umpire in the particular sport include safeguarding the well being of the participants and the age of the players.

---

10 For a further rugby case see Allport v Wilbraham [2004] EWCA Civ 1668, in which the issues at trial were limited to ones of fact, it being common ground that if the referee had failed to call 'engage' or had done so when the front rows of each side were not yet in the correct crouched position, then the claimant would have succeeded.

11 Supra, n.1.

(2) THE LIABILITY OF THE SPORTS COACH

Similarly, a duty of care is also owed by the sports coach who controls and supervises the performance of sporting games and events. Their position may be said to be analogous to that of the referee or umpire insofar as they have control over how the game or training is performed and to undertake some responsibility for the safety of the player, given that those players are taking instruction and guidance from the coach and may often be less skilled or experienced than that individual.

It is not uncommon for such cases to be brought on behalf of child claimants injured during the course of sporting activity in which, once more, the standard of care required of the coach may be set by reference to the inexperience of the participants under supervision and the risks that they are or are not likely to appreciate. Once more it assists to consider the circumstances of the cases in which liability has been established.

Inadequate instruction

In Gannon v Rotherham Metropolitan Borough Council,[12] a schoolboy successfully brought proceedings against a local authority in respect of failures on the part of a physical education teacher in failing to provide sufficient instruction before allowing him to dive into a swimming pool and against an amateur swimming association for failing to issue appropriate guidance to instructors. The first defendant had provided basic guidance as to the correct technique to be performed when diving from a diving block but then permitted the claimant to dive into the shallow end of the pool, which resulted in him breaking his neck.

Selection of opponent in training

In Hopkins v Pullen & Taylor (t/a Ippon Judo Club),[13] a claim was brought by an adult novice judo participant against his coach and club. The claimant had not participated in judo previously and was paired with an opponent who was up to 2 stones heavier than him and who

12 6 Feb 1991, Halsbury's Laws MR 91/653 (unreported elsewhere).

13 8 Dec 2005, Holland J., LTL 20/3/2006 (unreported elsewhere).

was also a novice. The claimant sustained a fractured clavicle as the weight of his opponent was applied when the claimant was not lying flat on his back. The existence of a duty of care was admitted but the breach disputed. It was held that the evidence demonstrated that the claimant had been shown how to perform the manoeuvre, including how to hold and fall. Having considered and taken account of expert evidence it was held that no breach of duty was made out on the facts. While there was said to be a limit to the size and weight disparity that was appropriate, that had not been exceeded on the facts of the case. The fact that the participants were novices was a relevant consideration when determining what standard of care to apply in respect of the conduct of the coach.[14]

Failure to remove from the activity

In Davenport v Farrow,[15] a successful junior athlete brought proceedings against his coach for alleged failures to heed complaints made by the claimant of back pain. Those symptoms were later discovered to be associated with spondylolysis. It was accepted by the defendant that a duty of care was owed to the claimant and admitted that if made out on the facts then the coach would have been in breach of duty. The claim failed on factual causation however, with the claimant's condition being found to have existed prior to the coach being engaged by the athlete and that as such the symptoms experienced did not arise as a result of a negligent failure on the part of the defendant.

Failure in supervision

In Woodland v Maxwell & Essex County Council,[16] a swimming teacher and a lifeguard were held responsible for the failure to supervise a 10-year old claimant during the course of a swimming lesson and for

14 See also Affutu-Nartoy v Clarke, Times, Feb 9, 1984, in which a school teacher who took part in a game of rugby with 15-year-old schoolboys was liable when the plaintiff suffered injury when he was tackled by him.

15 [2010] EWHC 550 (QB).

16 [2015] EWHC 273, [2013] UKSC 66 and [2015] EWHC 820 (QB) (part 20 proceedings).

failing to notice that she had gotten into difficulty, the consequence of which was that she suffered a brain injury. In an earlier application brought by the local authority to strike out the claim brought against it the Supreme Court had held that the local authority owed a non-delegable duty of care to the claimant, overturning the decisions below and as such the local authority was also held liable for the claimant's injury.

In Bacon v White & Chartfield Associates,[17] an adult novice scuba diver on her first open water dive off Chesill Beach, Dorset, failed to apply the training that she had been given and descended to the bottom of the seabed without her buddy. The first defendant who was supervising lost sight of the deceased. She was later found on the seabed at a depth of 13 metres without her breathing apparatus 3-4 minutes later. She was taken toe the surface but could not be revived. It was held that once the deceased had descended the first defendant's duty was to ensure that she was safe. While he had other duties owed to other divers he was found to have been negligent in looking away from the deceased and losing sight of her. The standard of care owed by the first defendant was held to have been higher as a result of the inexperience of the deceased and the dangerousness of the activity being undertaken.

Duty to advise of the risks and to insure

In Van Oppen v Clerk to the Bedford Charity Trustees,[18] a school pupil, aged 16, was injured whilst playing in an inter-house rugby match at Bedford School. A claim was brought on the basis that there had been a failure to coach or train the schoolboy in proper tackling techniques, but also as there had been an alleged failure to advise or warn the boy's parents of the risks of injury during a game of rugby, that the school had no insurance in respect of the risk of injury or that the boy's parents should arrange for insurance. The claims were dismissed at trial and an appeal was pursued in respect of the insurance claim. The Court of Appeal dismissed the appeal on the basis that the school/pupil relationship did not give rise to a duty to consider the pupils' economic welfare and it would not be fair, just and reasonable to

17 May 21, 1998, QBD, LTL 22/5/98 (unreported elsewhere).

18 [1990] 1 WLR 235, CA.

impose a duty in such circumstances. It was also concluded that in any event the boy's parents had not relied on the school to advise them as to what insurance they should or should not have taken out.

Simple failures in the execution of the activity

Finally, the individual under supervision may suffer injury simply because of a failure in the execution of the activity by the supervisor. Thus, in Woodroffe-Hedley v Cuthbertson,[19] a claim was brought under the Fatal Accidents Act 1976 on behalf of the infant son of the deceased who died in a climbing accident on Mont Blanc. The defendant was the deceased's guide and was an experienced alpine climber. During the ascent the defendant became concerned at the heat of the sun on the ice above them and decided to move to an area that was in the shade. Instead of making a two-screw belay to secure himself as the leading climber he made only one. As he ascended a large sheet of ice broke away under his feet and dragged him down, the force of his fall on the rope attached to the deceased dragged the deceased down, the rope caught on a rocky outcrop and the deceased was killed. The court found the defendant to have been negligent in dispensing with the second screw and in not using a running belay. The court observed that mountain climbing is extremely dangerous and anyone who climbs with a guide is to be treated as consenting to the ordinary dangers of mountain climbing, however it is also the duty of the guide to minimise the risk of injury or death and in that respect the defendant had failed to discharge his duty.

---

19 June 20, 1997, QBD, Dyson J., LTL 5/9/97 (unreported elsewhere).

CHAPTER SIX
LIABILITY OF THE GOVERNING BODY

INTRODUCTION

In this chapter we consider the potential liability of the sporting governing body or licensing authority based upon a direct duty of care being owed by that authority to the participant, since the existence of such a duty was acknowledged in certain circumstances in 2001. A governing body may also be responsible for the acts and omissions of its agents or employees in vicarious liability, which is discussed elsewhere in this book in more detail.[1]

LIABILITY OF THE GOVERNING BODY

Direct duty owed by the governing body

Since the decision of the Court of Appeal in the case of Watson v British Boxing Board of Control,[2] it has been acknowledged that sporting governing bodies may owe a duty of care to participants in sporting events in cases where, by reason of those bodies exercising a regulatory function involving the imposition of rules and regulations relating to the safety of the participant, they may assume responsibility for their safety.[3] The sporting cases in which a duty has been held to arise have generally involved the sports in question being ones in which there is an inherent risk of injury, although a large number of different sports carry with them their own particular inherent risks.

The decision in Watson arose out of the injuries sustained by the professional boxer, Michael Watson, during the WBO super-middleweight

---

1 See Chapter 8.

2 [2001] QB 1134, CA.

3 Previous claims advancing such allegations had failed. Cf. Agar v Hyde [2000] 201 CLR 552, in which the claimants' claims that the International Rugby Football Board owed a duty to participants to amend the rules of play to remove unnecessary risks associated with scrums, was unsuccessful.

world title fight against Chris Eubank in London in September 1991. The claimant sustained a subdural haemorrhage as a result of sustaining a blow to the head in the fight. As a result of the lack of availability of adequate equipment or trained personnel at the ring side there was a critical delay in the claimant receiving the necessary management of his head injury. The claim was defended on the basis that no duty of care was owed to the claimant and that in any event the claimant's condition would not have been improved, even had such equipment and trained personnel been available to treat him immediately. The match was held under the rules and regulations imposed by the defendant Board, which included a requirement that promoters comply with prescribed safety arrangements which included the presence of three doctors in attendance at the ringside. No resuscitation equipment was provided however and the doctors who were present were not trained in how to use that equipment.

At trial, Kennedy J. heard expert evidence that the standard response to subdural bleeding was to intubate, ventilate, sedate and paralyse the patient as soon as possible and to administer appropriate drugs. As a result of the inadequate assistance at the ringside, that standard procedure was not followed until the claimant reached hospital, some 25 to 30 minutes after his collapse in the ring. The court found that had the necessary medical equipment and personnel been present at the ringside then the claimant would have been treated appropriately within three minutes of his collapse and he would have found himself in a materially better condition. The trial judge went on to find that the Board owed the claimant a duty of care, despite the fact that it did not itself organize the bout nor did it have any contractual involvement, because the Board permitted such fights to take place where the safety arrangements that *it* imposed were complied with. That was said to establish a sufficient nexus between the claimant and the Board as to justify imposing a duty of care, where the risk of injury was clearly foreseeable. When considering whether it was fair, just and reasonable to impose a duty, the court took account of the fact that boxers, as a class of individuals, are unlikely to have a well-informed concern for their own safety. In contrast, the Board was considered to be a body with particular or special knowledge, which gave advice that it knew would be relied upon.

It was acknowledged that the decision represented a development of the law in this area but the court found that it was a gradual development and one that it was appropriate to take. Breach of duty was established on the basis that there was no good reason why the Board had not required appropriate medical assistance to be available and as no consideration had been given to introducing a standard response to subdural bleeding. The Board sought to raise *volenti non fit injuria* as a defence.[4] The court rejected that defence on the basis that while the claimant had consented to the risk of injury at the hands of his opponent, he had not consented to the risk of injury as a consequence of the defendant's failure to ensure that appropriate safety arrangements were in place.

The Board appealed to the Court of Appeal, where duty of care, breach and causation were all the subject of further argument. The Court of Appeal also acknowledged that the decision broke new ground, but observed that the case was unique, with distinctive features that took it outside the previously established categories of duty of care in negligence. The Court of Appeal held that the trial judge had been correct to observe that it was difficult for the Board to express a particular concern for the safety of participants and to take steps to regulate it, but then to deny that the duty of care contended existed. It was said that the traditional concept of neighbourhood where there was a clearly foreseeable danger of the potential for physical injury was authority for the trial judge's decision.[5]

The Court of Appeal also noted that boxing was unusual in that it was one of only a few sports where the object was to cause physical injury to the participants and it was said that could not have survived as a *legal* sport without strict regulation, which was provided by the Board, the

---

4 See Chapter 10 for a further discussion of the defence of *volenti non fit injuria.*

5 Citing Perrett v Collins (1998) Times, June 23, 1998, [1999] PNLR 77, in which the claimant suffered injury when an aircraft crashed and when the defendant had negligently certified the aircraft as being in airworthy condition. Hobhouse LJ considered that there was sufficient foreseeability and proximity to impose a duty of care, the need for proximity having been satisfied by the fact that the defendant had a, *"measure of control over and responsibility for a situation, which if dangerous, will be liable to injure the claimant".*

aim of which was to limit the injuries inflicted during the course of the bout. The regulations were noted to include those designed to ensure that a boxer received appropriate medical treatment once injured. Everyone involved in the sport was required to comply with the Board's rules and regulations and as such it was held that the Board assumed the responsibility of identifying and defining the nature of the medical assistance that should be provided at matches. The duty was not to take reasonable care to avoid causing personal injury, but to ensure that participants who sustained injuries were properly treated and was one imposed on the Board to require that they make regulations imposing on others a duty to achieve a particular result and did not require that the Board itself provide the medical facilities that it required be in place. The act of undertaking to cater for the medical requirements of a victim of injury was said to generally carry with it a duty to exercise reasonable care in accommodating those requirements. The Board's position was distinguished from that of a volunteer who might offer assistance at the scene of an accident. It was observed by Lord Phillips that the authorities established that:

> *"These cases establish that, where A advises B as to action to be taken which will directly and foreseeably affect the safety or well-being of C, a situation of sufficient proximity exists to found a duty of care on the part of A towards C. Whether in fact such a duty arises will depend upon the facts of the individual case ... "*[6]

On the facts of the case it was held that as the Board made provision in its rules for medical precautions and made compliance mandatory, a relationship of sufficient proximity arose between the Board and its members who were professional boxers.[7] The claimant was considered to belong to a class over which the Board had control and it was responsible for a situation liable to result in injury to him if it did not exercise reasonable care. Policy arguments were raised as to the absence of insurance held by the Board and as to the fact that the Board was non-profit making, however those were not sufficient to avoid the

6 At paragraph 72.

7 At 1146.

finding of the existence of a duty of care. The defendant's appeal was therefore dismissed.

It has been suggested in other works that the duty is likely to arise only where the governing body assumes a regulatory rather than an advisory role[8] and that successful claims against governing bodies are likely to be rare.[9] Certainly Lord Phillips drew a clear distinction in Watson between the giving of advice and the making of regulations,[10] in stating that:

> *"In my judgment there is a difference in principle between making rules and giving of advice, but it is not one which assists the board. Had the board simply given advice to all involved in professional boxing as to appropriate medical precautions , it would be strongly arguable that there was insufficient proximity between the board and individual boxers to give rise to a duty of care. The board, however, went far beyond this. It made provision in its rules for the medical precautions to be employed and made compliance with these rules mandatory."*

In cases decided since Watson, the question of whether the role of the governing body in question was more advisory or regulatory has been considered to be important in the determination of whether a duty of care was owed. Ultimately, the additional ingredient where a party exercises a regulatory role rather than a purely advisory role is one of control. The additional element of control was a determinative feature in the case of Wattleworth v Goodwood Road Racing Company Limited.[11]

In Wattleworth, the deceased was an experienced national and international rally and motor racing driver who was participating in an

8 Beloff et al, *Sports Law*, 2nd edition, p150-151 at n5.63.

9 Ibid, at n.5.64.

10 At p1161, paragraph 82.

11 Elisabeth Ruth Wattleworth (Widow & Administratrix of the Estate of Simon Wattleworth, deceased) v (1) Goodwood Road Racing Company Limited (2) Royal Automobile Club Motor Sports Association Limited (3) Federation Internationale De L'Automobile [2004] EWHC 140 (QB).

amateur track day taking place on a racing track that was owned and managed by the first defendant, Goodwood. During the course of a race the deceased crashed his car into a wall of lorry tyres adjacent to an earth bank and he died as a result of his injuries. The second defendant, MSA, was the national body with power to license motor racing venues within the United Kingdom and was an affiliate of the third defendant, the FIA, which governed international competitive motor racing. Any venue that held international events would be inspected by personnel of the FIA. Shortly before the day on which the deceased died and prior to an unrelated international event, experts from the MSA and the FIA had advised Goodwood as to safety precautions that should be taken. Once implemented those safety measures were subsequently re-inspected by officers of the MSA and FIA. In addition to advancing a claim as against Goodwood as occupiers of the venue the claimant contended that a duty of care was owed by the MSA and the FIA arising from their inspections of the track and in respect of the advice given to Goodwood with regard to track safety and in the issuing of a track licence. The claimant's case alleged negligent design or selection of the tyre fronted earth bank. Goodwood successfully argued that in adhering to the safety recommendations imposed by the MSA and the FIA and in taking and relying on expert advice, it had discharged the duty that it owed to the deceased to take reasonable care.

The MSA were held to owe a duty of care to the deceased, notwithstanding that the event at which the deceased suffered fatal injury was not one for which an MSA track licence was required, on the basis that it was the party principally responsible for track safety. Davis J. said:

> *"...in using the circuit Mr Wattleworth, in common with other lawful users, was entitled to assume and would have assumed that all due care had been exercised by the persons – whoever they be – who had undertaken responsibility for safety matters."*[12]

And also:

> *"...in my judgment, on the facts here, the MSA assumed a responsibility going well beyond the mere authorisation of events for which*

12 Paragraph 118.

an MSA Track licence and event permit was required. In my view, the MSA ... was plainly giving advice to Goodwood both as to the circuit and as to the protective devices to be deployed around the track, when it contemplated and expected that such advice would be acted upon by Goodwood not only with regard to the MSA events but also with regard to other motor car uses of the circuit. It is plain to me ... that Goodwood itself did so rely on the MSA. ... [the MSA] had a measure of control in this context – for in practical terms what [they] said went."[13]

On the facts however, the duty that was held to have been owed by the MSA, was considered to have been discharged. Davis J. added that had the MSA disclaimed the assumption of responsibility then the responsibility for track safety would have been that of Goodwood.[14]

The court also concluded that the FIA owed no duty of care to the deceased as it was far less involved than the MSA in prescribing safety measures that should be in place at the venue, with its role being, in effect, exclusively advisory in nature. The distinction drawn between the FIA and the MSA was one of whether their role went further than being exclusively advisory and whether there was the additional element of control. Additionally, the court held that causation was not made out as the immediate cause of the deceased's fatal injuries was not found to have been the impact with the tyre wall which was the subject of criticism. Although not part of the ratio of the case the defence of *volenti* did not find favour, the court concluding that the deceased had consented to the risks associated with motor racing but had not consented to risks associated with a failure to take reasonable care to ensure that the track was safe so that if primary liability had been established, the defence of *volenti* would have failed.

The contrasting, non-sporting case of Sutradhar v Natural Environment Research Council,[15] is another example of a case in which the role of the defendant was purely advisory. There the British Geological Survey, a

13 Paragraph 120.

14 Paragraph 125.

15 [2006] UKHL 33.

department of the defendant, had prepared a report assessing the hydro-chemical character of the aquifer units of central and northern Bangladesh and the possible toxicity of groundwater to fish and to humans. The claimant developed symptoms of arsenic poisoning, brought proceedings contending that the tests undertaken by the defendant should have included ones for arsenic and arguing that the report gave the impression that no arsenic was present. The House of Lords held that there was no proximity between the parties as the defendant had no control whatsoever over the supply of drinking water in Bangladesh nor was there any legislation, contract or other arrangement that imposed on the defendant any responsibility for ensuring that the water was safe to drink.

A further illustration of the advisory role not being sufficient to bring about the imposition of a duty of care notwithstanding that the advice was provided in respect of participant safety is that of Agar v Hyde.[16] In that case two claimants suffered serious back injuries as a result of collapsed scrums in the course of playing rugby. Proceedings were brought against the International Rugby Board on the basis that the rules of play were not framed adequately to reduce an obvious risk of injury. While the claimants succeeded at first instance the Court of Appeal of New South Wales concluded that no duty was owed as the relationship between the IRB and the players was too remote in that the rules were directed at a body of players and officials over whom the defendant had no control. Quite apart from the advisory/regulatory distinction, the decision in Agar v Hyde may also be explicable on the basis that it is one thing to fail to make provision for the prevention or treatment of an injury that is common to a particular sport, whereas it is quite another for liability to arise for injury more generally despite the provision of in-game safety rules on the basis that those rules are inadequate.

In the case of Biddick v Morcom,[17] the question was considered of whether it is necessary to demonstrate *reasonable reliance* on the

16 Agar v Hyde [2001] HCA 41.

17 The Personal Representatives of the Estate of Cyril Biddick (deceased) v Mark Morcom [2014] EWCA Civ 182.

involvement of the defendant by the claimant. In Watson and Wattleworth clearly there had been reliance by the claimant and the deceased respectively, in the form of their participation, upon the parties responsible for the relevant safety features in each case. Watson and Wattleworth were considered by the Court of Appeal and it was observed that the cornerstone of the duty in these cases was ultimately the assumption of responsibility and that a claimant was not required to prove such actual reliance. On the question of reliance, in Wattleworth, Davis J. had noted that, "*...while reliance was important in the Watson case, I do not think the lack of specific reliance here is of itself dispositive of the question of whether a duty of care was owed...*",[18] commenting that in Perrett v Collins,[19] there had been no such direct reliance as the claimant was unaware of the inspection that was the basis of the finding that a duty was owed to him by the defendant.

In Biddick, an elderly homeowner who has having his loft insulated had offered to stand beneath a hinged loft hatch so as to ensure that it remained closed. He left his post following which the claimant sustained injury when the loft hatch opened, the catch working loose as a result of vibration from drilling above. When considering the question of the need to prove reliance, McCombe L.J. observed that:

"There is no need to import any element of "reasonable reliance" in such a case, as might be required in a case of economic loss, in order to lead to the existence of a duty of care. Once Mr Biddick took upon himself the task of ensuring that the latch remained closed it seems to me that he assumed a duty to perform that task carefully, even if Mr Morcom did not see Mr Biddick's role as an element in his own safety."[20]

Vicarious liability

The liability of a governing body might also arise in circumstances where the individual primarily responsible for the injury of the sportsperson is someone for whom the governing body is vicariously

18 Paragraph 118.

19 Times, June 23, 1998, [1999] PNLR 77.

20 Paragraph 53.

liable, such as a sports umpire or referee[21] or an inspector responsible for ensuring that standards of safety set by the governing or licensing body have been complied with. A further detailed discussion of the circumstances in which vicarious liability may arise can be found elsewhere in this work.[22]

The liability of the governing body in the future

Since the decision in Watson sporting governing bodies have increasingly been brought into proceedings, with defendant organisers seeking to pass on liability with the argument that they relied on safety requirements laid down by their licensing authority or governing body.

The trend of bringing in a governing body as a party to such a claim is likely to continue with sportsmen and women, who bring claims against organisers of sporting events finding their task somewhat more difficult by virtue of the amendment of section 47(2) of the Health & Safety at Work Act 1974, introduced by section 69 of the Enterprise and Regulatory Reform Act 2013. Claimant sportsmen and women who pursue those responsible for the condition of the course or track or for equipment located or positioned upon them no longer have available to them allegations based on the breach of strict statutory duties.[23] The sportsman may therefore also look to the governing body for redress, placing reliance on the extent to which the safety of the track or course and its furniture is regulated by the governing body.

An illustration of the effect of the change brought about by section 69 of the 2013 Act can be found in Hide v The Steeplechase Company (Cheltenham) Ltd & Ors.[24] In that case the claimant was a jockey who was injured when his horse fell during a steeplechase at Cheltenham.

21 As in Vowles v Evans v Welsh Rugby Union Ltd [2003] EWCA Civ 318.

22 See chapter 8.

23 Previously, s.47(2) of the Health & Safety at Work Act 1974 Act provided that breaches of health and safety legislation gave rise to civil liability and to a private right to compensation as a result. The effect of s.69(1) Enterprise and Regulatory Reform Act 2013 was to reverse that presumption of civil liability for breach of a statutory duty enacted under the 1974 Act.

24 [2013] EWCA Civ 545.

Having jumped a hurdle the horse stumbled and veered to the right, throwing the claimant towards a guardrail which ran around the track. The upright posts of the guardrails were padded for about twenty yards beyond each hurdle and were approved by the British Horseracing Authority. The claim was brought against the management of the race-course relying largely on regulation 4 of the Provision and Use of Work Equipment Regulations 1998, which provided that work equipment should be so constructed or adapted as to be suitable for the purpose for which it is provided. The regulations provided that *"suitable"* meant *"suitable in any respect which it is reasonably foreseeable will affect the health and safety of any person"*. At first instance the court held that the railings were *"suitable"* within the definition provided by the regulations but had imported the concept of *"reasonable foreseeability"* was applied as if the regulation imposed a standard identical to that at common law. Overturning that decision, Longmore L.J. observed that, "*The European Directives and therefore the Regulations exist in a world different from the common law*", and that, *"it seems to me that it must be for the defendant to prove that any relevant accident was due either to unforeseeable occurrences beyond the defendant's control or to exceptional events the consequences of which could not be avoided in spite of the exercise of all due care. So construed the Regulation will be consistent with the Directive.*" Thus, liability arose under the regulations on those facts where it would not have done at common law. Following the change brought about by the Enterprise and Regulatory Reform Act 2013, the decision at first instance would have stood and it follows that the task of the claimant sportsperson is now more difficult in such a claim brought against the organizer of the event. It seems likely now that all such cases involving injury after 1 October 2013 will be decided purely on common law principles that the claim against the governing body as well as against the organizer will become a more familiar scenario.

Whether liability may arise based on a direct duty or in vicarious liability, ultimately the governing body would be well advised to ensure that it carries appropriate and sufficient insurance against the risk posed by such claims.[25]

---

25 As is discussed in Kevan et. al., *Sports Personal Injury: Law and Practice*, 2002, at paragraph 10.29 and Chapter 25.

CHAPTER SEVEN
LIABILITY OF THE CLUB DOCTOR

INTRODUCTION

This Chapter hopes to provide a brief introduction to the basic principles of medical negligence. Although the majority of personal injury claims in the sports law context involve injuries sustained on the pitch, there is ample scope for such claims to also involve medical negligence. Medical negligence in the sports law context can involve negligent advice and treatment (including a failure to diagnose or a failure to advise of drug side effects) by clubs, coaches, physiotherapists or club doctors. Beyond clinicians employed or instructed by the club, an athlete may suffer negligent treatment whilst in hospital or while attending his or her general practitioners following an injury on the pitch.

DUTY OF CARE

This is unlikely to cause much difficulty, as a doctor/treating clinician invariably owes the patient a duty of care. It is worth noting this duty only arises should the doctor assist or the doctor is under a duty to accept the patient, for example a person who attends at hospital. There is no duty on a doctor attending a sports game as a spectator to intervene.

STANDARD OF CARE: BOLAM TEST

The case of *Bolam v Friern Hospital Management Committee*[1] sets out the usual rule (referred to as the Bolam test) for assessing the appropriate standard of reasonable care in negligence cases involving skilled professionals such as doctors, physiotherapists, pharmacists etc. The standard of care must be in accordance with a responsible body of opinion, even if others differ in opinion, i.e. whilst the treatment may not be optimal, it will not be negligent if there is a body of responsible doctors who would have done the same.

---

1 [1957] 1 WLR 582.

THE PLAYER'S RESPONSIBILITY – CONTRIBUTORY NEGLIGENCE

Contributory negligence may arise if a player was injured in part due to their own actions. Damages may be reduced to account for this. This is dealt with in more detail in Chapter 10.

Contributory negligence arguments in clinical negligence claims are usually quite rare. However, the commercial pressures involved in sports can lead a player to minimise his or her injury in order to continue playing. For example, clubs engaging in sport involving potential head injuries will often ask their athletes undertake an assessment at the beginning of each year/season which provides a baseline for cognitive responses. After a potential head injury, the player will be asked to perform some cognitive tests to ascertain the impact of the head injury. Players who are found to have deliberately underperformed in order to set a lower baseline are likely to be found to be contributory negligent.

If a player fails to undergo a medical assessment or fails to engage with the medical treatment, his award may well be reduced.

CAUSATION

Causation is determined by the standard "but for" test, that is, "but for" the defendant's negligence, would the claimant's loss have occurred. If the answer is yes, there is no factual causation. So if a claimant's damage would have occurred in any event, even if treated appropriately by a doctor, causation will not be established.

Lord Hoffmann in *South Australia Asset Management Corp v York Montague Ltd*[2] gave a classic example.

> *"A mountaineer about to undertake a difficult climb is concerned about the fitness of his knee. He goes to a doctor who negligently makes a superficial examination and pronounces the knee fit. The climber goes on the expedition, which he would not have undertaken if the doctor had told him the true state of his knee. He suffers*

2 [1996] UKHL 10.

an injury which is an entirely foreseeable consequence of mountaineering but has nothing to do with his knee."

In this case, the doctor's duty extended to preventing harm being caused as a result of the knee injury, not as a result of external events, such a rock fall. Although it was foreseeable that someone might be injured climbing, the knee injury did not cause it on this occasion.

EXCEPTIONS TO THE GENERAL RULE ON CAUSATION

The standard 'but for' test requires proof, on the balance of probabilities, that but for the negligence the damage would not have been caused. In any claims against a club's medical personnel, the basic 'but for' test will apply. However, the area of medical negligence often throws up difficult causation problems and courts have developed a variety of ways to address some of these by modifying the standard 'but for' test.

There are special rules applying to claims arising from exposure to asbestos (*Fairchild v Glenhaven Funeral Services* [2002]).

Material contribution (multiple cumulative causes)

If there are a number of causes which could each have solely caused the injury and medical evidence was unable to show which if them caused the injury, the claimant will be unable to discharge the burden of proof,[3] i.e. it is not possible to say on the balance of probability that the tortious act caused the injury.

However, if the number of causes all materially contributed to an indivisible injury, the claimant will be able to establish causation.

The application of the rule in clinical negligence cases was considered by the Court of Appeal in *Bailey v Ministry of Defence*[4]. The claimant aspirated her vomited due to her being in a weakened state, leading to a cardiac arrest and hypoxic brain damage. The weakened state was party

---

3 *Wilsher v Essex Area Health Authority,* [1988] AC 1074.

4 2008 EWCA Civ 883.

as a result of negligent care following an operation and partly as a result of pancreatitis (non-negligent). The Court of Appeal approved the lower court's findings that both pancreatitis and the Defendant's negligence had been causative in the Claimant's weakness. However, it was not possible to say, on the balance of probabilities, that the negligent care led to the weakness, only that it provided a material contribution.

The Court of Appeal stated that a more than *de minimis* contribution was enough to modify the 'but for' test in some case:

> *"[...] If the evidence demonstrates that 'but for' the contribution of the tortious cause the injury would probably not have occurred, the claimant will (obviously) have discharged the burden. In a case where medical science cannot establish the probability that 'but for' an act of negligence the injury would not have happened but can establish that the contribution of the negligent cause was more than negligible, the 'but for' test is modified, and the claimant will succeed."*

Doubling of the risk

As noted above, usually one must prove that one the balance of probabilities the tortious act caused the damage. However, the balance of probabilities can sometimes be satisfied by proof that the negligence more than doubled the background risk so is the 'most probable' cause. This issue was raised in the mesothelioma context in *Sienkiewicz v Greif*[5].

However, the Privy Council[6] has recently provided some obiter guidance on the 'doubling of risk' test in deciding questions of causation. It suggested "caution" against the use of the "doubling of risk" test but acknowledged that it can sometimes be "very helpful"

---

5 [2011] UKSC 10.

6 *Williams v The Bermuda Hospitals Board* [2016] UKPC 4.

RESTRICTIONS ON CAUSATION

Proving 'but for' causation is necessary but not sufficient in order to succeed in liability; the rules on legal causation may prevent a successful claim. These rules are generally applicable to all torts.

Acts of third parties/Breaking chain of causation

An act of a third party or a supervening act may break the chain of causation, if it was not foreseeable and not a direct result of the initial negligence. Therefore, if a doctor fails to recognise that a player suffered a concussion and, as a result of the concussion the player loses consciousness after the game and falls down stairs, the doctor will be liable for the player's injuries. However, if the player suffers a bleed in his brain, which will be fatal within days, but is killed in a road traffic accident immediately after the game, the chain of causation is likely to be broken.

SCOPE OF THE DUTY

The court will have to ask what is the scope of the duty of which the Defendant is in breach and does place limitations upon the Defendant's liability. Although similar, this concept differs from remoteness.

Lord Bridge said in *Caparo v. Dickman*[7]:

> *"It is never sufficient to ask simply whether A owed B a duty of care. It is always necessary to determine the scope of the duty by reference to the kind of damage from which A must take care to save B harmless"*.

Therefore, if the doctor failed to diagnose a knee injury and, as a result of the clear bill of health the player takes part in a game, the doctor cannot be liable for the consequences of a violent tackle which results in a facial injury. The purpose and scope of the doctor's duty was not to prevent the player participating in the game, but to prevent further injury as a result of his original knee injury.

7 [1990] 2 AC 605 (HL).

CONSENT

The clinician is under a duty to seek consent before proceeding with treatment. This is a fundamental duty as any interference with a person's bodily integrity is technically an assault or battery unless consented to[8]. When assessing the issue of consent, the law has moved a long way from the position of 'the doctor knows best'; it is now the case that the patient's wishes must factor strongly in any clinical decision. Medical decisions should be made *with* the patient rather than *for* the patient.

The most significant case in this area in recent years is the Supreme Court case of *Montgomery v Lanarkshire Health Board*[9] which marked a clear change in how courts assessed whether informed consent had been obtained. The issue in this case was whether the option of a Caesarian Section should have been discussed with a high-risk diabetic mother in circumstances where there was a very small risk of serious injury to the child through a natural delivery. The doctor's evidence was that she did not discuss this risk with diabetic women as they would invariably elect for a caesarean section given the potential impact upon the child and it was *'not in the maternal interests for women to have caesarean sections'*.

The Supreme Court disagreed with this approach and emphasised that all doctors are under a duty to take reasonable care to ensure that their patient is aware of any "material risks" involved in any recommended treatment and of any reasonable alternatives. When assessing whether something is material, it is for the court to look at the particular circumstances and assess whether a reasonable person in the patient's position would be likely to attach significance to the risk, or the doctor is (or should be) reasonably aware that this particular patient would be likely to attach significance to the risk.

In order to bring a successful personal injury claim the test is whether, had the patient been properly informed, they would not have undergone the procedure. If the patient would not, the injury resulting

8 And will allow a claimant claim for aggravated damages.

9 [2015] UKSC 11.

from the procedure is causally linked to the failure to inform the patient.

In the sports law context, it is imperative that athletes are properly informed of all material risks, which would include those that may impact on their future performance. Doctors know that athletes are very likely to attach significance to any risk that would even slightly reduce their performance and will need to ensure their consent process includes an exposition of these risks.

Obtaining informed consents in the sports context can present particular challenges. If the doctor/physiotherapist is an employee of the club, tension may arise between what is best for this individual player and what is best for the club. Sadly, there have been cases of clubs sacrificing an athlete's future health for their own short-term gain. The San Francisco 49ers were found liable for fraud and ordered to pay damages for failing to tell Charlie Krueger about the severity of a knee injury[10]. The team doctors administered regular pain-killing drug injections without telling him about the true condition of his knee, the adverse impact of the injections and the prospect of permanent physically disablement.

The athlete may also hold back information if it potentially impacts on their chance of playing or obtaining a new contract or may prefer immediate medical treatment to continue the game despite the significant risk of future severe irreparable damage. It has not been uncommon for players to deliberately underperform at their cognitive testing at the start of the season in order to avoid any noticeable deterioration when they are retested after a head injury. Treating clinicians must be alive to the risk of minimisation by the athlete and hold a full dialogue about the proposed treatment, taking positive steps to ensure he or she understands all the material risks.

The fact that the player is a child does not automatically mean they cannot provide informed consent. Clearly, if the child is very young, a parent or guardian will have to provide consent instead. Much will depend on the circumstances and the age of the child. In *Gillick v West*

---

10 189 Cal.App.3d 823 (Cal. Ct. App. 1986).

Norfolk and Wisbech AHA[11], it was held that a child under 16 could provide consent without the parents being informed. The court was influenced by the fact that the child in question had sufficient maturity and intelligence to understand the nature and implications of the proposed treatment.

Club doctors cannot avoid their duty to obtain informed consent by not putting appropriate testing in place ensure they are aware of the full extent of a player's physical impairments. If a club fails to perform sufficient diagnostic tests, they cannot rely on their own lack of awareness when obtaining informed consent. The case of *Radwan Hamed v Mills & Tottenham Hotspurs FC Ltd*[12] illustrates this. Tottenham Totspurs sent their player, Radwan Hamed, for a routine cardiological check-up which included an echocardiogram and an electrocardiogram. Although these tests raised a suspicion of a latent and potentially fatal heart condition known as hypertrophic cardiomyopathy, his condition was not explored further. He should have had a comprehensive cardiological check. Neither he nor his parents (he was 17 at the time) ever realised that there was a small chance he might suffer a cardiac arrest if he continued playing football.

The defendants in that case tried to argue that even if Radwan had been fully consented (i.e. informed of the risk of a cardiac attack), he would have continued to play. However, they discontinued this defence after emotional evidence from his parents to the effect that they would never have allowed their son to be exposed to this risk, had they been fully informed.

A year after these tests, he had a cardiac collapse during a match and suffered irreversible brain damage. Both the club and the cardiologist were held to be negligent; the club doctor had failed to pick up on the suspicions the cardiologist had tried to communicate and the cardiologist because he failed to follow up on his recommendation for a clinical review.

---

11 [1986] AC 112.

12 [2015] EWHC 298 (QB), 16 February 2015.

This case emphasises the importance of having proper diagnostic protocols in place and open and clear channels of communication between the club's clinicians and outside medical professionals.

CONCUSSION

Concussions (also known as a mild traumatic brain injury) are all too common in contact sports and result from a knock or jolt to the head. This issue has emerged as a hot topic in recent years as the science and medical knowledge surrounding this issue has grown. Concussions can be difficult to detect but they can lead to serious and permanent injury if left untreated. The injury caused by a concussion can be greatly exacerbated if the player continues to play, especially if the player suffers a further injury. The issue of concussions from sports injuries has been explored in detail in other works but it is worth mentioning briefly.

Clubs have a responsibility, as far as is reasonably practicable, to ensure the health and safety of their players. Professional clubs will be expected to have protocols in place for ensuring that any concussive injuries are properly diagnosed, assessed and treated. Protocols set down by professional clubs may include cognitive pre season testing, tests and methods for reaching a diagnosis and the various treatment options available which will include the appropriate resting time depending on the severity of the injury. For example, the International Rugby Board has introduced the Head Injury Assessment protocol which includes a ten minute assessment procedure, a compulsory online module for players, coaches and officials and mandatory concussion management training for medical staff. The management of confirmed and suspected concussion is also subject to an independent review by at least two experienced independent medical practitioners.

In terms of the club doctor's involvement, it will be for them to make the clinical decision as to whether the player has suffered concussion and when it is safe for them to return to play. The club doctor has a duty to exercise his clinical judgment taking into account the protocols he receives from the club and guidance/directives from the applicable governing body. The club doctor's duty, when assessing and treating concussion, will be to the player – he or she cannot allow the commercial considerations of the club to factor into his clinical decisions. Some professional clubs will employ completely independent doctors to assess their players given that club doctors may sometimes display bias – either consciously or sub consciously – towards the club.

Ideally, all clubs should adopt the following steps:

(1) Compulsory education around the fact that concussion is a brain injury, the risks it poses, both short-term and long-term, and general concussion management. This education should aim to create an atmosphere where concussion is taken seriously.

(2) Consider having an independent doctor assess and manage concussion.

(3) Carry out risk assessments on the health of each player, which specifically record the history of previous concussion.

(4) Keep records for each player of any concussion injuries.

(5) Have robust policies and protocols in place for the assessment and management of concussion.

(6) Include in their disciplinary policy sanctions for failing to adhere to the club's policy or protocol on concussion

CHAPTER EIGHT
VICARIOUS LIABILITY

INTRODUCTION

The law regarding vicarious liability has been developing rapidly in recent years, making it easier for claimants to sue defendants for torts committed not only by their employees but also for torts committed by individuals not actually employed by the defendant. Given the quite dramatic widening of the scope of vicarious liability recently, and the use to which it can be put in the sports context, it was thought useful to devote a chapter to explaining the new developments in this area.

VICARIOUS LIABILITY

In contact sports, all participants owe a duty of care to one another. In order to show a breach of that duty, conduct must be reckless and fall below the standard required of a reasonably skillful and competent professional player. It must be an act that is more serious than an error of judgement. Thereafter, the injury suffered must be foreseeable. For example, it must be the type of injury that one would expect from a foul or tackle.

What happens if a player/referee/club official or other participant injures a player, either through negligence or deliberate assault? He or she will be personally liable and can be sued in tort (either in negligence or for trespass against the person). Players can sue other players, the referee, coaches and governing bodies. If the player is a highly paid professional, a claim can be brought directly. However, if the defendant is only an amateur player or a semi professional, a more solvent tortfeasor may have to be identified as there is little merit incurring the costs of obtaining judgment if the defendant has no assets against which to enforce it.

By contrast, the club is likely to have more significant assets and insurance. It is usually more attractive to bring an action in vicarious liability against the club for the transgressions of one of its players.

The extent to which the defence of volenti is applicable in sports negligence cases has been discussed in Chapter 10. The application of this defence will be equally applicable to vicarious liability as it is to the direct liability of the players.

Traditional employment cases and acts

Courts have, for some time, imposed vicarious liability where the defendant is an employee of the club and the tortious act was, without question, an integral part of his or her employment, for example a dangerous tackle or challenge resulting in an injury which went beyond that to which the player could have given his implied consent by stepping on to the field of play.

The High Court, in the case of *Elliott v Saunders and Liverpool Football Club*[1] first accepted that in principle a professional football club could be vicariously liable for the acts of its employees who negligently caused injury to another player. However, in this case, the claimant, Paul Elliott, failed to prove there had been a breach of the duty of care by Dean Saunders regarding a tackle that ended his career. Accordingly, no vicarious liability was imposed.

In *McCord v Swansea City and Cornforth*[2] the High Court went further and held that it was appropriate to impose vicarious liability on Swansea City Football Club, the employing club, for a dangerous tackle which left Brian McCord's with severe lower leg injuries. However, there is no real mention or discussion of vicarious liability in the judgment.

Extending the ambit of vicarious liability in sports law cases

However, what of deliberate acts that, ostensibly, are not connected to the game, for example a player who assaults another in the car park after a match, or acts perpetrated by players who have not signed a contract of employment with the club? Historically, it would not have been possible to bring a claim for vicarious liability for intentional torts or where the club did not formally employ the player.

---

1 Unreported, English High Court, 10 June 1994.

2 (1996) The Times, 19th Dec.

In relation to intentional torts, the House of Lords eventually, and dramatically, overruled this line of authority[3] by focusing on the '*close connection*' between the tort and the individual's employment. Lord Steyn, stated the real question was whether the employee's wrongdoing "*was so closely connected with his employment that it would be fair and just to hold the employers vicariously liable*". By focusing on this test of close connection, framed against the notions of fairness and justice, the House of Lords created a new precedent in holding an employer vicariously liable for the intentional torts of their employees.

The imposition of vicarious liability, therefore, involves a two stage test:

(a) Stage one involves an inquiry into whether the nature of the relationship between the club and the tortfeasor (player) is such that the principles of vicarious liability might attach.

(b) Stage two involves an inquiry into the connection between the club and the tortious act or omission of the tortfeasor.

Stage One: Nature of the Relationship

In terms of the first stage, if there is an employment relationship, i.e. the club employs the player, the first stage test will clearly be met. This raises the question of amateur and semi-professional players, who do not have a contract of employment with the club.

Until recently, it was felt it was difficult to bring a claim vicarious liability unless there was a formal employment relationship between the defendant player and the club. Although the High Court imposed vicarious liability on a club for an amateur referee for his decision during an amateur game in the case of *Vowles v Evans*[4], the Court of Appeal, in a later decision, appeared to warn against this approach. In *Gravil v Carroll & Redruth RFC*[5] considered the potential vicarious liability of a rugby club for a punch thrown by one of its semi-professional players. Although the club was found vicariously liable, their Lordships

3 *Lister v Hesley Hall Ltd,* [2001] UKHL 22.

4 [2002] EWHC 2612 (QB).

5 [2008] EWCA Civ 689.

stressed that the judgment was not intended to apply to the playing of sports where no contract of employment exists. Some commentators felt this amounted to ban on imposing vicarious liability for sports injuries where there was no employment contract.

However, matters have moved on and recent judicial movements mean that courts are now willing to impose vicarious liability outside the employment relationship.

The Supreme Court in *Various Claimants v Catholic Child Welfare Society*[6] and the Court of Appeal in *JGE v. The Trustees of the Portsmouth Roman Catholic Diocesan Trust*[7], have broadened the scope of vicarious liability to include relationships which are 'akin' to an employment relationships. In both these cases, a diocese was held vicariously liable for abuse by a brother monk and a priest, respectively, despite there being no contract, terms, conditions, wages, or right of dismissal except through the Church in Rome.

In *JGE,* it was held that vicarious liability can attach to relationships which are "*akin to employment*". Ward LJ in that case concluded that a relationship between bishop and priest was so close in character to one of employer/employee that it was "*just and fair to hold the employer vicariously liable*".

In *Various Claimants v Catholic Child Welfare Society,* Lord Phillips highlighted five policy reasons which "*usually make it fair, just and reasonable to impose vicarious liability on the employer*": "*(i) the employer is more likely to have the means to compensate the victim than the employee and can be expected to have insured against that liability; (ii) the tort will have been committed as a result of activity being taken by the employee on behalf of the employer; (iii) the employee's activity is likely to be part of the business activity of the employer; (iv) the employer, by employing the employee to carry on the activity will have created the risk of the tort committed by the employee; (v) the employee will, to a greater or lesser degree, have been under the control of the employer.*" (paragraph 35)

---

6 [2012] UKSC 56.

7 [2012] EWCA Civ 938.

He added (at paragraph 47):

> *"... I have identified those incidents of the relationship between employer and employee that make it fair, just and reasonable to impose vicarious liability on a defend- ant. Where the defendant and the tortfeasor are not bound by a contract of employment, but their relationship has the same incidents, that relationship can properly give rise to vicarious liability on the ground that it is 'akin to that between an employer and an employee'"*

Ultimately Lord Phillips considered the relationship between the teaching brothers and the Institute was "*sufficiently akin to that of employer and employees to satisfy stage 1 of the test*"[8]. The Institute conducted its activities as if it were a corporate body; the teaching activity and even the entering into of contracts with the managers, was undertaken because the Institute required it; the teaching activity was in furtherance of the Institute's "*mission*"; and the "*manner in which the brother teachers were obliged to conduct themselves as teachers was dictated by the Institute's rules*".

In *A v Trustees of the Watchtower Bible and Tract Society*[9] abuse by a 'voluntary' ministerial servant was found to satisfy the vicarious liability test. The abuser had been a Jehovah's Witness ministerial servant.

Stage two: connection between the club and the tortious act or omission of the tortfeasor

As noted above, whilst the traditional position was that an employer could not be liable for intentional torts, the courts have reversed this position in the case of *Lister v Hesley Hall Ltd*[10].

Egregious torts have found to be still have the requisite connection when assessing the stage 2 test. In *Various Claimants v Catholic Child*

---

8 para 60.

9 [2015] EWHC 1722.

10 [2001] UKHL 22.

Welfare Society[11] and *JGE*[12] it was held that sexual abusing children was sufficiently linked to the positions entrusted to the tortfeasors. It is clear, therefore, that even if an employee misused the position entrusted to him to commit the tortious act, this will not prevent vicarious liability being established, despite the presence of specific rules set down by the club prohibiting test behaviours.

Recent guidance on vicarious liability

The Supreme Court has revisited the basis of and test for vicarious liability in twin judgments; the first stage of the test was considered in *Cox v Ministry of Justice*[13] and the second stage in *Mohamud v WM Morrison*[14].

In *Cox* the relevant relationship was between a prison and a prisoner who was working in the prison kitchen. Whilst working in the kitchen the claimant was cleaning up a spillage when a prisoner dropped a sack of rice onto her back and injured her. The judge at first instance did not find the relationship between the prison and prisoner was akin to employment as the prison authorities were legally required to offer work to prisoners. It was, therefore, not a case where two parties were in a voluntary relationship in which each acted to their own advantage. However, the Court of Appeal allowed the appeal on the basis that the work performed by the prisoner was done on behalf of the prison service and for its benefit.

The Supreme Court in Cox found that not all the five factors identified by Lord Philips had equal significance. It emphasised that the factors regarding insurance and control did not have the significance which they were considered to have in the past. Although the absence of even a "*vestigial degree of control would be liable to negative the imposition of vicarious liability*", it was not likely to be a factor of "*independent significance*" in most cases.

11 [2012] UKSC 56.

12 [2012] EWCA Civ 938.

13 [2016] UKSC 10.

14 [2016] UKSC 11.

The remaining three factors identified by Lord Philips were:

> *"...(ii) the tort will have been committed as a result of activity being taken by the employee on behalf of the employer; (iii) the employee's activity is likely to be part of the business activity of the employer; (iv) the employer, by employing the employee to carry on the activity will have created the risk of the tort committed by the employee..."*

The Supreme Court considered that these factors were inter-related and formed the basis for identifying the circumstances in which vicarious liability might be imposed outside formal employment relationships; their applicability was not confined to certain category of cases.

Applying Lord Phillips' criteria to the case of *Cox* the Supreme Court found that activities assigned to prisoners such as the provision of meals, although not commercially motivated, were an integral part of the activities which the prison service carried on in furtherance of its aims. The prison authorities had placed the prisoner in a position where there was a risk that he may commit a variety of negligent acts within the scope of activities assigned to him. He was also required to work under the direction of prison staff. Accordingly the court held the prison authorities to be vicariously liable for the prisoner's negligence.

In the context of the potential liability of sports organisations, it is of note that the Court in *Cox* emphasised that the defendant did not need to be carrying on activities of a commercial nature and the benefit derived from the tortfeasor's activities did not need to take the form of profit. It was sufficient that the defendant's interests were being furthered by the tortfeasor. This clarification is of particular note in the context of cases involving the negligence of amateur sports participants (e.g. a dangerous tackle or a misguided referee decision).

Therefore, on the basis of recent judicial guidance, it is clear that sports organisations can be held to be vicariously liable for volunteer, amateur and semi professional participants. Although the questions of whether vicarious liability should be imposed will be factually specific, if a club directs a referee how to act or provides guidance to marshalls at games, it may well be the case that it will be held to be vicariously liable for any breaches of duty. This is particularly the case if the club is professionally run at a profit, selects the amateur participant, provides the premises and sets down rules of conduct or tactics. Although amateur participants are not paid to play, they may receive free or subsidised uniform or coaching and it is arguable that the club has control over their behavior in that there is the threat of sanction or substitution should a participant not adhere to the club rules or direction. The case *may* be very different if it involved an amateur club, with only basic organisation and run mainly by volunteers.

The area of vicarious liability is "*on the move*"[15] and the law has moved a long way from the apparent immunity afforded to clubs for volunteers by Gravil.

The second of the Supreme Court cases, *Mohamud*, was concerned with the second limb of the test for vicarious liability. In *Mohamud*, the claimant was attacked in the forecourt of a petrol station by an employed attendant. The lower court and Court of Appeal held that the attendant's duties were limited in that they did not involve the possibility of confrontation or being placed in a position where violence was likely. The fact that his duties involved interactions with customers was not enough for there to be a sufficiently close connection between what the attendant was employed to do and the assault.

The Supreme Court restated that the applicable test was the '*close connection'* test set down in Lister v Hesley Hall[16] and although it conceded the test could be "*imprecise*" this was "*inevitable given the infinite range of circumstances where the issue of vicarious liability arises"*.

However, the Supreme Court did elaborate upon the application of the test; two matters must be considered. Firstly, what functions or "*field of activities*" have been entrusted by the employer to the employee, i.e. what was the nature of his job. This had to be assessed broadly. Secondly, was a sufficient connection between the position in which he

---

15 *Various Claimants v Catholic Child Welfare Society,* [2012] UKSC 56, at para. 19.

16 [2002] 1 AC 215.

was employed and his wrongful conduct to make it right for the employer to be held liable.

The Supreme Court held that the assault was "*within the 'field of activities' assigned to him*" and was part of a "*seamless*" episode. When telling the claimant not to return to the premises, he was purporting to act on behalf of his employer. Although it may have been a gross abuse of his position, it was in connection with the employer's business which was to serve customers. The decision of the Supreme Court simply reinstates the established first stage test for vicarious liability, what is surprising was the lower courts' initial decisions: if sexual abuse can meet the second stage test, it is unclear why it was viewed that a physical assault on an adult would not.

In the sports law context, clubs and organisations should remember that the courts will adopt a "*broad approach*" to whether the tortious act was within the "*field of activities*" assigned to the employee. The Supreme Court has shown itself more and more ready to make the link between the tortious act and activity the tortfeasor was engaged in. The justification used by the Supreme Court in Mohamud was that the assault followed on from the initial engagement to become a "*seamless act*". This raises the prospect of vicarious liability being attributed for an attack in a car park immediately following a game where words were exchanged between players.

The case of *Mohamud* echoes the rational of the Court of Appeal in *Mattis v Pollock*[17] which involved a nightclub bouncer who, after an altercation, went back to his flat to obtain a knife and returned to the club and stabbed the claimant in the back in revenge: the Court of Appeal held there was a "*direct link to the events*". Assaults off the pitch, for example on a referee in relation to a controversial decision or against another player, may well attract vicarious liability.

Evidence gathering

Given the prospect of vicarious liability being imposed on clubs, it would be prudent for clubs and associations to have a robust system in

17 [2003] 1 W.L.R. 2158.

place for accident investigations.

Should an accident or assault take place on or off the pitch, it is advisable to gather evidence as soon as possible, rather than try to piece together what happened once litigation has been intimated. Although not exhaustive, the following steps should be taken:

- prepare a note or incident report and include as much detail as possible

- request a statement from anyone involved in the incident, any witnesses and the referee (if the incident happened on the pitch).

- take and record contact details of any eye witnesses.

- retain any video footage recording the incident.

CHAPTER NINE
ABUSE IN SPORTS LAW

INTRODUCTION

Unfortunately, sexual abuse has been only too prevalent in the area of sports law. Whilst no sport condones or lends itself to sexual abuse, the power dynamics and the intimacy involved in the coach/athlete relationship too often lead to opportunities to abuse and a corresponding lack of opportunity to disclose.

The issue of sexual abuse of athletes has been recognized by the International Olympic Committee, which issued a Consensus Statement[1] in 2007, reporting that:

> *"...sexual harassment and abuse happen in all sports and at all levels. Prevalence appears to be higher in elite sport. Members of the athlete's entourage who are in positions of power and authority appear to be the primary perpetrators. Peer athletes have also been identified as perpetrators. Males are more often reported as perpetrators than females...Research demonstrates that sexual harassment and abuse in sport seriously and negatively impact on athletes' physical and psychological health. It can result in impaired performance and lead to athlete drop-out. Clinical data indicate that psychosomatic illnesses, anxiety, depression, substance abuse, self harm and suicide are some of the serious health consequences.*
>
> *The risk of sexual harassment and abuse is greater when there is a lack of protection, high perpetrator motivation and high athlete vulnerability (especially in relation to age and maturation)."*

Athletes come from many different culture and familial backgrounds and are often isolated from their family and peers as a result of the geographical location of training or competitions. Athletes are usually young, required to spend substantial amounts of time with their

---

1 https://stillmed.olympic.org/Documents/Reports/EN/en_report_1125.pdf

coaching staff and compete in incredibly pressured and isolated competitive sporting environments. The act of coaching may well involve physical contact. The power difference in and intensity of the relationship may prevent victims from disclosing the abuse or recognising the inappropriateness of the perpetrator's conduct.

There is no specific legislation which regulates the area of sexual abuse in sport.

In terms of criminal law, any sexual activity between adults and with children under 16 is generally illegal and constitutes abuse. The Sexual Offences Act 2003 targets sexual activity committed by those in positions of trust. Although the offences cover all children under 18, they are principally designed to protect young people who, even though they are over the age of consent for sexual activity, are considered vulnerable to sexual abuse and exploitation.

This includes sexual activity and relationships with adults who hold a position of trust, responsibility or authority in relation to them and, as a result, have a considerable amount of power and influence in their lives. The law defines specific roles and settings where sexual activity between 16 and 17 year olds and those in positions of trust, responsibility or authority constitutes a criminal offence. Currently being a coach/official in a sports club is currently is not considered under the law as a specified role.

CAUSES OF ACTION

It is trite to state that identifying correct cause of action in the civil case from the outset is fundamental but it is particularly necessary with these type of claims. As abuse can take many forms and can lead to a multiplicity of problems with the victim, one may need to be inventive about which causes of action are relied upon.

Trepass to the person

Trepass to the person requires the intentional or reckless infliction of injury, or the threat of it. If a child is sexually abused or physically hit, or feared the same, then this will amount to trespass to the person.

Negligence

However, not all tortious acts against children will amount to a claim for trespass to the person. Children can sometimes be subject to emotional harm or oppression. The law of negligence can be employed in circumstances where perpetrator's behavior falls short of a deliberate assault. Coaches are under a duty to take reasonable care when imparting their knowledge and skill to their athletes. If a young athlete suffers psychiatric harm from an overly grueling regime put in place by a coach, this may amount to negligence. If an 18 year old enters into an ostensibly consensual sexual relationship with his or her coach, this may amount to negligence if the coach knew or ought to know that the athlete was very vulnerable and he was in a position of trust.

Wilkinson v Downton type claim (intentional infliction of harm)

Where deliberate acts fall short of trespass to the person, it may be possible to bring a *Wilkinson v Downton*[2] claim. This type of claim involves an "*act willfully done which was calculated to and did cause physical harm to the claimant*". Physical harm will include psychiatric harm. In that case the defendant told the claimant, as a 'joke', that her husband had been seriously injured, which caused her to suffer nervous shock.

Although the use of *Wilkinson v Downton* claims has waned, it can still be a useful tool given not all sexual abuse involves touching or an assault. In the case of *C v D*[3], it was alleged that the defendant videoed the claimant naked in the shower and, on another occasion, pulled down his trousers and stared at his buttocks. The High Court appeared to accept that these were deliberate acts and could be actionable on the basis of *Wilkinson v Downton* but the principle only allows recovery for a recognised psychiatric injury; it does not allow recovery for emotional distress[4].

---

2 [1897] EWHC 1 (QB), [1897] 2 QB 57.

3 [2006] EWHC 166 (QB).

4 Mr Justice Field, at para 94.

Lord Neuberger [5] has recently provided guidance as to when a statement, which causes distress to a claimant, would be considered to be actionable:

> *"In order to decide when a statement, which is not otherwise tortious, and which causes a claimant distress, should be capable of founding a cause of action, it is necessary to bear in mind five points, some of which are in tension. First, that there must be circumstances in which such a cause of action should exist...Secondly, given the importance of freedom of expression.... it is vital that the boundaries of the cause of action are relatively narrow. Thirdly, because of the importance of legal certainty...the tort should be defined as clearly as possible. Fourthly, in the light of the almost literally infinite permutations of possible human interactions, it is realistic to proceed on the basis that it may well be that no set of parameters can be devised which would cater for absolutely every possibility. Fifthly, given all these factors, there will almost inevitably be aspects of the parameters on which it would be wrong to express a concluded view, and to let the law develop in a characteristic common law way, namely on a case by case basis."*

Breach of Statutory Duty

A claim may arise if Parliament has imposed a statutory duty upon a party to carry out a particular function and a claimant suffers injury as a result of a breach of this statutory duty. Chapter 3 covers some of the more common statutory duties that might apply in the sports context, e.g. Health and Safety at Work Act 1974 and Occupiers' Liability Act 1957 etc.

The most common type of claim in the area of abuse will be against a local authority regarding its duties towards children.

Human Rights Act 1998

It may be possible to bring a claim under the Human Rights Act, where the abuser is a public servant, such as a care worker. This type of claim

5 *Rhodes v OPO*, [2015] UKSC 32.

would usually involve alleging a breach of Articles 3 (protection from torture and oppression) and 8 (right to privacy) of the European Convention on Human Rights would be relevant. The limitation period is only 1 year, with a discretionary extension.

Data Protection Act

Sometimes abuse may include taking inappropriate photographs or videos. Photographs and images of individuals, which are be classified as "personal data", are regulated by the Data Protection Act 1998.

Unlike negligence, damages under the Data Protection Act 1998 will include damages for distress. Although the claim for damages is only triggered if there has been financial loss, courts have shown themselves to be flexible about this requirement. The fact that a child needs therapy as a result of these photographs being taken may well be sufficient, if this is obtained privately.

The Protection from Harassment Act 1997

The Protection from Harassment Act 1997 prohibits harassment, i.e. a course of conduct (i.e. on at least 2 occasions) which amounts to harassment of another. It is not specifically defined in the Act but includes causing anxiety or distress.

A person is taken to know that conduct is harassment if "*a reasonable person in possession of the same information would think the course of conduct amounted to harassment of the other*"[6].

Section 3 of the Act allows a civil remedy for harassment which sounds in damages. The standard of proof required is on the balance of probabilities, rather than the criminal law standard.

This Act has been used successfully in the sporting context. *In Levi v Bates*[7], two previous directors, Mr L and B, of Liverpool United Football Club had publicly fallen out. B published (by articles in

---

6 Section 1.

7 [2015] EWCA Civ 206.

match-day programmes and through the club's radio station, operated by Yorkshire Radio) his version of the dispute. Two of these publications intimated that fans of the club should contact Mr L directly, published his home address and may have allowed some fans to see his telephone number.

At first instance, Mr L's wife did not succeed as some publications were not targeted directly at her and therefore, in relation to her, there was not a 'course' of conduct. On appeal, it was held that it was not a requirement of the statutory tort of harassment that the claimant be the target of the perpetrator's conduct and, therefore, there was a 'course' of conduct as there had been two articles inviting fans to contact their home in a hostile manner.

Vicarious liability

As has been noted in Chapter 8, courts are gradually expanding the ambit of vicarious liability to allow for compensation in a variety of new situations, including abuse.

Non-delegable duties

Public authorities may be sued directly if an independent external contractor breached a non-delegable duty. In a groundbreaking judgment, the Supreme Court held that an education authority could be liable for an injury caused during a swimming lesson when the external contractor, negligently performed its duties[8].

The claimant was a pupil at a local authority school who got into difficulties while swimming. Unfortunately, he was rescued too late and suffered a hypoxic brain injury. The authority had not been supervising the child at the swimming lesson but had, quite reasonably, left this to the swimming centre and the lifeguard on duty. However, it was held that since any proven negligence occurred in the course of the very functions which the school had assumed an obligation to perform and delegated to its contractor, the educational authority was in breach of duty as the duty was non-delegable.

8 Woodland v Essex County Council [2013] UKSC 66.

Therefore, depending on the circumstances, local authorities may be liable for any negligence which is committed by its contractor during the running or supervision of a sporting activity.

LIMITATION

The difficulties surrounding disclosure abuse are becoming more recognised, not least by the courts which have been adopted a more favourable approach to compensation for abuse. It has been increasingly recognised that sexual abuse is usually accompanied by secrecy and threats against disclosure. Reporting is often difficult; either due to the age of the victim or feelings of shame or embarrassment. These factors will make it more difficult for a victim to bring a claim within the usual time limits.

The case of *A v Hoare*[9] has eased limitation difficulties. Prior to this case, claimants only had 6 years with which to bring a claim for a deliberate assault. This caused real difficulties for victims of sexual abuse who faced a much stricter limitation regime than victims of negligently inflicted personal injury. The Supreme Court (then House of Lords) overruled previous case law and held in *A v Hoare* that intentional torts will no longer be subject to the strict time limit of six years, and instead will be subject to the three year extendable time limit as used for personal injury claims.

Therefore, in a claim for sexual abuse, the primary limitation period is either three years from the date of accrual of the cause of action or the 'date of knowledge' whichever is the later[10]. The date of the accrual of the cause of action would normally be the date when the claimant suffered damage.

Section 14 of the Limitation Act 1980 defines 'date of knowledge' as the date upon which the claimant first had knowledge of the following facts:

(a) that the injury was significant;

9 [2008] UKHL 6.

10 Limitation Act 1980, s 11.

(b) that it was attributable to the act or omission which is alleged to constitute negligence, nuisance or breach of duty; and

(c) the identity of the defendant or, where the act or omission was that of a person other than the defendant, the identity of that person, and the additional facts supporting the bringing of an action against the defendant.

A claimant has the requisite knowledge when he or she knows enough to make it reasonable to begin to investigate whether he or she has a case against the defendant[11].

The test is an objective one and, in accordance with Section 14(3), the claimant will have imputed to him or her knowledge that one might reasonably have been expected to acquire from facts observable and ascertainable by him or her; or from facts ascertainable with the help of medical or other expert advice. Lord Hoffman in *A v Hoare* stated the application of Section 14(2) "*assumes a practical and relatively unsophisticated approach to the question of knowledge*".

Section 33 of the Limitation Act 1980

However, even a court finds that a claimant did acquire the relevant knowledge about their injuries more than three years ago, the court has a broad discretion under Section 33 to disapply the three year limitation period.

The claimant's reasons for not commencing proceedings earlier, including the claimant's psychological state and its inhibiting effect, will be relevant to the Court's exercise of discretion under Section 33.

The discretion is wide and unfettered and courts can decide to hear oral evidence and not just rely on the paperwork. A number of factors will be taken into account, including when the complaint was first made and with what effect, whether it was recorded and whether there were any convictions for the abuse.

---

11 *AB v Ministry of Defence* [2009] EWHC 1225 (QB), [2009] All ER (D) 54 (Jun).

The Court must consider all the circumstances, including any prejudice to the defendant. This involves considering what evidence might have been available to the defendant if a trial had taken place earlier or the defendant had learned of the claim earlier. A defendant is very likely to argue that it has been prejudiced by the delay in bringing these proceedings and a fair trial will not be possible due to the passage of time/loss of evidence.

The strength of the evidence available to the parties will also be relevant to the exercise of discretion. If the abuser has been convicted, this will be very strong evidence in favour of the court exercising its section 33 discretion. The potential corroborative evidence of other victims would be a factor in a claimant's favour in terms of both liability and limitation.

A helpful exposition of how courts approach the question of its section 33 discretion is set out in the judgment of Mrs Justice Swift in the case of *Raggett v The Society of Jesus Trust 1929 for Roman Catholic Purposes & Anor*[12]. Very broadly, three factors help will influence the court; (i) whether a fair trial is still possible, (ii) what are the reasons for the delay and (iii) where does the balance of prejudice lie.

There is separate provision made for claimants who were under a disability[13] or lacked capacity[14] at the time of the tort. Time does not run whilst the claimant is a child (i.e. until 18 years of age).

CAUSATION

The consequences of childhood abuse and neglect can be devastating. The long-term effects can impact upon the physical, psychological, cognitive, and behavioral development of children.

The legal principles governing proof of causation of damage are the same as those generally applicable to personal injury claims. However, whilst there has been a greater acceptance and awareness in recent years

12 [2009] EWHC 909 (QB).

13 Section 28(1) and section 28(6).

14 Section 38(3).

of the potential impact on victims, proving causation poses difficulties in claims involving the abuse of a child.

The importance and impact of the particular timing, intensity, and context of abuse on the outcome is still unknown[15]. While it is known that factors such as the age, intelligence, family background of the child generally impact upon the outcome, these factors may cause differing effects from child to child. Further, some maladaptive coping strategies may only come to the fore much later on, for example when the child is an adult or in times of stress, or may have a unique effect on a particular child.

The further difficulty is trying to explore the extent of the damaged suffered, i.e. when trying draw a picture of how the child would have developed and functioned but for the abuse. The abuse is often perpetrated before the child's personality has fully formed. Therefore, there is no clear picture what the child's personality would have been like as an adult or how he or she would have performed educationally. A child who has been abused is often left more vulnerable to further abuse at the hands of another perpetrator.

When bringing a claim for compensation, the claimant must be careful to tease out these difficulties in causation. Expert evidence will assist in this regard – a psychiatrist will be able to diagnose any psychiatric disorders and attribute causation of these. It may also be useful to compare the child's educational and employment achievements to those of his or her siblings and parents (who have not been abused).

QUANTUM

Claims for compensation in abuse cases will usually involve both general damages and special damages.

General Damages

A claimant will be entitled to an award for general damages for the immediate effect of the abuse that he or she endured, and for the long-

15 *Understanding Child Abuse and Neglect*, National Research Council (1993).

term difficulties (usually psychiatric but sometimes physical) which they experienced as a result of that abuse. The usual tariff system for personal injury will be of some assistance[16] in cases involving sexual abuse but specific quantum cases are heavily relied upon and provide greater guidance. Quantum cases in this area are increasing along with the volume of claims and the following cases will provide some guidance as to the level of awards available for these type of cases (this is not an exhaustive list):

Various Claimants v Bryn Alyn Community (Holdings) Ltd (In Liquidation)[17]

Claimant v D

Various Claimants v Flintshire County Council[18]

MAGA v Trustees of the Birmingham Archdiocese of the Roman Catholic Church[19]

AB and Others[20]

Raggett v The Society of Jesus[21]

However, it should be noted that some of these cases are old, not all contain a very detailed discussion of quantum and some of the Claimants were not found to be fully credible.

16 Judicial College's '*Guidelines for the Assessment of General Damages in Personal Injury Cases*'.

17 (2003) EWCA Civ 85, (2003) QB 1441.

18 [2001] EWCA Civ 302.

19 [2010] EWCA Civ 256.

20 [2010] EWHC 1005

21 [2012] EWHC 3132.

Special Damages

In abuse claims, the most common categories are loss of earnings/vulnerability on the labour market, cost of therapy/counselling and care and assistance. It is worth exploring in this chapter the more unusual heads of special damages which can be claimed in abuse claims.

Treatment costs

These usually relate to psychiatric symptoms and the psychiatric expert should recommend specific treatment, with costings provided. A claimant will be entitled to the entire cost of any recommended therapy if liability and causation is established, rather than a percentage of the costs of therapy depending on the exact attribution. This is because in order for therapy to be successful, a claimant will normally have to undergo the entire treatment[22].

Expenditure on alcohol

It has been recognised by courts that abuse can trigger substance abuse due to the claimant struggling to deal with the effects and memory of the abuse and, therefore, self-medicating. If the medical evidence shows that the claimant drank or used legal substances (e.g. cigarettes) excessively, than the excess expenditure may be recoverable.

However, this type of claim can be difficult to bring. The leading case is *Eagle v Chambers* regarding excessive[23] consumption of cigarettes. The court held "if the medical evidence were to convince the court that the accident had caused such injury to the brain that the victim had no real choice but to increase her consumption of cigarettes, could the extra consumption be a head of damage". Therefore, it is a high threshold; the claimant must be deprived of a choice in deciding to consume the substance excessively.

---

22 *Various Claimants v Bryn Alyn Community (Holdings) Ltd (In Liquidation) Claimant v D* , [2003] QB 1441, paragraph 1441

23 [2004] EWCA Civ 1033.

In the case of *BJM v Eyre, Hawthorne, Loram and Riley*[24] the judge rejected the claimant's claim for the excessive expenditure on alcohol; the judge held that as the claimant was able to control his drinking in the past, he was able to exercise a choice and therefore, it was not recoverable.

Loss of familial support

Abuse can often lead to family breakdown for a variety of reasons. Sometimes the victim is not believed when they disclose the abuse, the impact of the abuse may means they isolate themselves from family members or the behavioural difficulties caused by the abuse can lead to fractured relationships. If the abuse caused a breakdown of the claimant's relationship with his or her family and has caused a financial loss, this can be recoverable. The most typical financial loss is the financial support or free accommodation that parents often provide to their children. In *C v D*[25], the claimant successfully claimed for some for the monies his parents would probably have paid towards his university education.

Care costs

The most usual claim for care in abuse cases is where the claimant's psychiatric condition causes them difficulties in performing their day-to-day activities. If this is attributable to the abuse, care costs will be recoverable.

Loss of Earnings

It will also be important to establish the extent of any causal link between the abuse and the Claimant's work capacity. Loss of earnings in the sports context has already been explored in Chapter 11. The Ogden tables should be the starting point if there are clear evidence of what the actual loss of earnings would be/ the pattern of his employment but for the abuse.

---

24 [2010] EWHC 2856.

25 [2006] EWHC 166 (QB)

Where a claimant is still employed but, owing to his injury, there is a risk he or she loses his or her job and will be unable to compete for alternative employment, a court may award a *Smith v Manchester*[26] award for "*handicap in the labour market*".

If there is no reasonable way to assess what the claimant's past and future lost of earnings, given the number of imponderables involved, a court may simply award the claimant a lump sum, assessed in a broad brush way (*Blamire*[27] award).

Aggravated and exemplary damages

These have been explored in detail in Chapter 11.

Compensation for committing a criminal act

If abuse happens at a young age, it is not uncommon for children to go off the rails and begin to offend. This type of claim is difficult as there are strong public policy considerations in play; where the claimant has acted illegally and the illegality is bound up within the claim, the court may dismiss the claim on this ground. Therefore, a Claimant cannot normally claim benefit from the commission of a crime.

In *Meah v McCreamer*[28] the Claimant was injured in a car accident, suffering brain damage as a result. He subsequently committed a number of acts of rape and malicious wounding, for which he was imprisoned for life. He sued the defendant, who was liable for the accident, arguing that he would not have committed those crimes but for the brain damage, and accordingly sought damages. Woolf J awarded him £60,000 in respect of his imprisonment.

However, in a subsequent case, Meah[29], he was not able to claim from the Defendant any indemnity for the compensation being sought by his victims.

---

26 (1974) 17 KIR 1, [1974] EWCA Civ 6.

27 *Blamire v South Cumbria Authority* [1997] PIQR Q1 CA.

28 [1985] 1 All ER 383.

29 (No 2) [1986] 1 All ER 943.

However, the Court of Appeal case of *Clunis v Camden and Islington Health Authority*[30] held that a claimant cannot be compensated for the consequences of his crime. As this case was decided post *Meah*, the dicta *Meah* must be in doubt.

The principle in the case of *Clunis* was adopted again by the Court of Appeal in *Worrall v British Railways Board*[31] in which the plaintiff alleged that an injury which he has suffered as a result of his employer's negligence had changed his personality. As a result, he had on two occasions committed sexual assaults on prostitutes, for which offences he had been sentenced to imprisonment for six years. He claimed loss of earnings while in prison and thereafter. The Court of Appeal struck out this claim. Mummery LJ said:

> *"It would be inconsistent with his criminal conviction to attribute to the negligent defendant in this action any legal responsibility for the financial consequences of crimes which he has been found guilty of having deliberately committed"*

Curiously, despite this line of authority, the Court of Appeal left open the door for compensation where a claimant has committed a crime as a result of a tortious act. In *Various Claimants v Bryn Alyn Community (Holdings) Ltd (in liquidation)*[32], it was stated:

> *"Notwithstanding anything said by this Court in Clunis an argument may survive that damages are recoverable in respect of tortious acts that have resulted in a law-abiding citizen becoming a criminal. However, there is no appeal with regard to this aspect of the claims either in respect of general damages or under the next head of claim to which we now turn, namely loss of earnings.*[33]"

However, the House of Lords followed *Clunis* in the case of *Gray v*

---

30 [1998] QB 978, [1998] 3 All ER 180, CA.

31 [1999] CA Transcript No 684.

32 [2003] EWCA Civ 85.

33 Para 131.

Thames Trains and others[34]. In that case the Claimant argued he committed manslaughter as a result of a Post Traumatic Stress Disorder caused by his involvement in a rail accident. He was convicted of manslaughter on the grounds of diminished responsibility. The defendant accepted liability to the claimant for his physical and mental injuries arising out of the accident. However, the House of Lords held that loss flowing from a sentence of the court could not be recovered, despite the fact that prior to the accident, the Claimant was a law abiding citizen in regular employment.

It, therefore, looks unlikely that any claim by a claimant for the consequences of his or her crime will be successful.

34 [2009] UKHL 33.

CHAPTER TEN
DEFENCES

INTRODUCTION

In this chapter we examine the various defences open to defendants in claims brought in the sporting context, including a consideration of what has been described below as consent by participation, *volenti non fit injuria*, contributory negligence and as to the possible availability of a contractual defence.

(A) CONSENT BY PARTICIPATION

(1) NEGLIGENCE

In the context of a claim brought in negligence the 'consent by participation' argument is, in short, an argument that by participating in the particular sporting activity the claimant consented to all of the usual risks of injury associated with it. Consent to risks beyond the usual hazards to be expected from the activity might be said to fall into the realm of *volenti*, which is discussed further below. While consent by participation is discussed here within the chapter dealing with defences as it is raised as a defence in almost every case in which a sportsperson may be the subject of proceedings brought against them by a fellow participant, often supplemented by the additional defences discussed below, the argument is in effect no more than the other side of the coin to the contention that there was no breach of duty at all. In his or her defence the defendant may contend (i) that the claimant consented to the usual risks and hazards associated with participation, (ii) that he or she was subjected to nothing more than such usual risks by the defendant's conduct and (iii) that there was no breach of duty as the standard of care applied to the defendant's conduct is set by reference to what the usual risks and hazards of the particular sport are.[1] Thus, if

---

1 For further discussion of this argument see Chapter 1, which deals in more detail with issues of standard of care in negligence. In Condon v Basi [1985] 1 WLR 866 and Rootes v Shelton (1968) ALR 33, it was suggested that the question of risks inherent in the activity arose for consideration at the duty rather than the breach stage.

the claimant is injured as a consequence of a common risk to be expected in the sport then not only did the claimant consent to those risks, but there will have been no breach of duty as the defendant will not have failed to come up to the relevant standard of care.[2]

Thus in Condon v Basi,[3] the point was expressed by Sir John Donaldson MR in terms that the risks affecting a participant in a game of football are quite different from those affecting someone taking a walk in the countryside. In Caldwell v Maguire,[4] it was noted that the standard of care was set by reference to the *"prevailing circumstances"* which included a consideration of the activity's *"inherent dangers"*. The defence of *volenti* outlined below might be considered to be simply an extension of the consent argument.

(2) TRESPASS TO THE PERSON

In a claim of trespass to the person the participant is again taken to consent to contacts that may reasonably be expected to occur in the course of the particular sport in question. Thus, in the case of a boxing match, neither participant would have a cause of action for injury suffered during the fight, despite the fact that they resulted from what might otherwise have been a battery. This is to be contrasted with consent to *"a savage blow our of all proportion to the occasion. The man who strikes a blow of such severity is liable in damages unless he can prove accident or self-defence"*.[5]

In the unusual case of Blake v Galloway,[6] the claimant, who was 15 years old, was participating with four friends in horseplay which involved throwing twigs and pieces of bark chipping at each other when

2 It has been suggested that liability would arise where a participant acted in a way to which the other participant could not have been expected to consent – Beloff et. al., *Sports Law*, 2nd edition, 2012, at 5.40, citing Ridder v Thaler (1990) unreported.

3 [1985] 1 WLR 866.

4 [2001] EWCA Civ 1054.

5 Lord Denning MR in Lane v Holloway [1968] 1 QB 379, 386-7.

6 [2004] EWCA Civ 814, [2004] 1 WLR 2844, [2004] 3 All ER 315, LTL 24/6/2004.

he was struck in the eye by a piece of bark. At first instance a district judge held the defendant liable in negligence, rejected a defence of consent to battery on the basis that the claimant had consented to participation in the game there had been no consent to injury to the face. The Court of Appeal considered that the principles discussed in Wooldridge applied as there was consensual involvement in an activity that involved the risk of physical contact, in which decisions were made quickly and instinctively and the nature of the activity made it difficult to avoid the risk of physical harm. It was held that the horseplay was conducted with tacitly agreed understandings and conventions, that there was no expectation that skill or judgment would be exercised and that there was a breach of duty only where the conduct amounted to *"a very high degree of carelessness"*. It was held that the error was one of judgment or a lapse of skill only and that there was no breach of duty in negligence. As regards battery it was held that the claimant had consented to being struck anywhere on the body and as such the claim should fail.

(B) VOLENTI NON FIT INJURIA

The maxim *volenti non fit injuria* encapsulates the principle that a party has given consent to what would otherwise be a breach of duty and has waived his or her right to bring proceedings in respect of that breach.[7] *Volenti* has been said to be relevant where there is consent to a lack of reasonable care rather than where there is consent to the risk of injury.[8] Where *volenti* applies, it amounts to a complete defence.

In consent by participation cases what is said is that simple participation in the activity implies acceptance of the risks inherent in it. In the case of *volenti* however the consenting party must go further in order that their consent can be said to apply to risks of injury brought about by failures to take reasonable care and agree to forego what would otherwise be a right to bring proceedings. What must be proved to establish such a defence have been said to include (i) consent to breach of duty, (ii) an agreement to waive a claim, (iii) the agreement must be

---

7 Clerk & Lindsell, 21st edition, Chapter 3, 3-95.

8 See Wooldridge v Sumner [1963] 2 QB 43 at 69, per Diplock LJ.

voluntary and not be due to compulsion, and (iv) the party consenting must first have full knowledge of the nature and extent of the risk to which they are consenting. Consent may be express but may also be implied, although it can be seen from the case law that the implication of consent to all of the features detailed above can be difficult to establish.

In the context of sporting activity in particular the defence of *volenti* has often been held to be of limited application on the basis that (i) the consent given by a participant is usually only to the usual risks inherent in the sport and no more, (ii) there is rarely agreement to waive any claim brought about due to any breach of duty that might arise, and (iii) where a risk that materializes has not been explained before any such consent is given, there was in any event a lack of knowledge of the nature and/or the extent of the risk, which vitiates any consent that may be found to have been given.

Thus, on this point in Wooldridge v Sumner,[9] a case in which a spectator was injured while watching an equestrian event, Lord Justice Diplock concluded that *volenti* was not relevant as the doctrine pre-supposed the commission of a tort by the defendant and because breach of duty had not been made out as the claimant had consented to the risks of injury normally associated with the sport and with his proximity to the action, in the absence of any reckless disregard by the defendant rider for the safety of spectators. Further, it was observed that the claimant had not consented to the defendant failing to take reasonable care, with full knowledge of the risks involved.

Similarly, in Smoldon v Whitworth,[10] the defence of *volenti* was rejected. In that case a player in an amateur rugby match brought proceedings against a referee who had failed to control a scrum resulting in the claimant sustaining a serious neck injury. The Court of Appeal held that the principle of *volenti* did not apply as the claimant had not consented to the referee's breach of duty. They observed that the claimant had not himself been a culprit in causing the scrum to collapse but if he

9 [1963] 2 QB 43 at 69.

10 [1997] PIQR P133, [1997] ELR 249, LTL 28/12/1996.

had been then a consideration of *volenti* as well as contributory negligence might be appropriate. The claimant was said to have consented to the ordinary risks of the game and also to have participated in the knowledge that the game would be regulated by the rules of the game framed to protect him and other players and which rules the defendant was required to apply.

In Blake v Galloway,[11] the Court of Appeal concluded that the claim in negligence was not made out as the parties had consented to the risks associated with everything except the consequences of a very high degree of carelessness. As such the Court of Appeal did not deal with whether a defence of *volenti* acquitted the defendant of liability for what would otherwise have been negligence. The issue of consent to injury was considered within the context of the claim of battery.

In King v Redlich,[12] the claimant was an amateur hockey player who was injured by a ricocheting puck struck during pre-match warm up session when the claimant had failed to wear a helmet. The shot was described as having been a normal one and within the reasonable expectations of the claimant. The claim was dismissed on the basis that the claimant had assumed and accepted the risk of injury during the warm up session, however it is notable that the defendant's conduct was not found to have been negligent and so acceptance of the risk of injury was not the reasoning that ultimately determined the outcome of the case.

Volenti also appears to be difficult to establish in the context of claims brought against organisers of sporting events. In White v Blackmore,[13] *volenti* was raised as a defence when a claimant brought proceedings on behalf of the deceased's estate, after the deceased died whilst watching a jalopy motorcar race organized by one of the defendants. It was noted that s.2(5) of the Occupiers' Liability Act 1957 expressly preserved the defence of acceptance of risk, but the defence of *volenti* failed as the deceased could not be said to have consented to risks created by the

11 Referred to above, [2004] EWCA Civ 814.

12 1985 782 (BC CA), [1984] 6 WWR 705, 30 CCLT 247.

13 [1972] 2 QB 651, [1972] 3 All ER 158, [1972] 3 WLR 296.

event organizer of which he was unaware. In Wattleworth v Goodwood Road Racing Co Ltd & Others,[14] the claimant brought proceedings on behalf of the estate of an amateur racing driver who died in a collision with a lorry tyre barrier during an amateur track day. The racetrack owner and the governing body advanced defences of *volenti*. It was held that had it been necessary to consider the defence, it would not have assisted the defendants, again as the deceased had consented only to the risks of motor racing and not to any breach of duty on the part of the defendants.

Where a claim is brought under the Occupiers' Liability Acts[15] in respect of activities freely undertaken by individuals on land belonging to others where the occupier has no involvement in the activities, *volenti* is likely to be prove more successful as a defence.[16] In Simms v Leigh Rugby Football Club Ltd,[17] the effect of s.2(5) Occupiers' Liability Act 1957 was that the claimant was found to have accepted the risks associated with the presence of a concrete wall running at a distance of just over 7 feet from the touchline of a rugby pitch belonging to the defendant, although the claim also failed for other reasons including that the claimant had not demonstrated that his broken leg had been due to a collision with the wall as opposed to being due to the tackle that drove him towards it, when such an injury was a known and accepted risk of such tackles in the game. There are other cases however in which the design of the venue has been responsible for injury, *volenti* has been held not to be available to the defendant occupier.[18]

In relation to sporting governing bodies, in Watson v British Boxing Board of Control,[19] it was held that *volenti* did not assist the sport's governing body as no consent had been given to lack of care in respect of

14 [2004] EWHC 140 (QB), [2004] PIQR P25, LTL 16/2/2004.

15 Section 2(5) Occupiers' Liability Act 1957 and Section 1(6) Occupiers' Liability Act 1984.

16 Tomlinson v Congleton Borough Council [2004] 1 AC 46.

17 [1969] 2 All ER 923.

18 E.g. Latchford v Spedeworth International, The Times, October 11, 1983, 134 NLJ 36, QBD.

19 [2000] ECC 141, Times, Oct 12, 1999, LTL 24/9/1999.

the provision of safety arrangements, for which the defendant was responsible.

In the sporting context then, arguments that rely on *volenti* and consent often stand or fall with (i) a determination of whether the risk that the participant consented to was an ordinary or expected risk of the particular sport, and (ii) whether the participant could be said to have truly consented to that additional risk of the defendant failing to take reasonable care, in full knowledge of the nature and extent of the risks. It has been said in other works that in the sporting context *volenti* will rarely be of relevance where the content of the duty and/or the standard of care have already been informed by the nature and extent of the risks accepted by the injured claimant.[20] It seems likely that arguments based on contributory negligence will prove more successful for defendants. As a partial defence, contributory negligence would also afford the court a greater degree of flexibility in its application, to suit the particular circumstances of the case.

(C) CONTRIBUTORY NEGLIGENCE

Contributory negligence generally

Contributory negligence may arise if the claimant was injured in part due to their own negligent act or omission. Damages may be reduced to reflect their own want of care. The party who pleads contributory negligence must prove it. The test for contributory negligent is objective.

Courts have a general power to apportion damages pursuant to the Law Reform (Contributory Negligence) Act 1945. This provides a partial defence. Section 1(1) provides:

> *"Where any person suffers damage as the result partly of his own fault and partly of the fault of any other person or persons, a claim in respect of that damage shall not be defeated by reason of the fault of the person suffering the damage, but the damages recoverable in respect thereof shall be reduced to such an extent as the court thinks*

20 Beloff et. al., Sports Law, 2nd edition, 2012 at 5.69.

just and equitable having regard to the claimant's share in the responsibility for the damage."

Therefore, the three key ingredients for assessing contributory negligence are:

1. fault of claimant;

2. if so, was this causative of damage;

3. if so, the extent to which it would be just and equitable to reduce damages.

In *Craven v Riches*[21], the defendant's duty of care extended to preventing faster riders from being obstructed by slower rider; it should not have allowed riders of different standards to use the track at the same time. However, the main cause of the accident was the claimant's careless riding and his damages were reduced by two-thirds.

In *Feeney v Lyall*[22], the claimant, a golfer, moved on to an adjacent fairway to recover a badly struck ball when he was struck by a ball hit from the tee of that fairway. Although he was unable to establish liability, the court indicated it would have reduced damages by 25% as he failed to check the actions of other golfers on the tee of the fairway he moved to.

In *Fowles v Bedfordshire CC*[23], the claimant suffered a serious spinal injury when he failed to perform a successful forward somersault. On appeal, it was held that the defendant was negligent because a youth worker employed by them had assumed the task of teaching the claimant how to undertake forward somersaults and, therefore, assumed a duty to make him aware of the risks and dangers. The youth worker did not instruct him properly, provide any warnings of the risks and allowed unsupervised access to the gym mats. However, the Court of Appeal found that there was contributory negligence; the claimant was

---

21 [2001] EWCA Civ 375; [2002] P.I.Q.R. P23.

22 1991 SLT 156.

23 Times, 22 May 1995; [1996] ELR 51; [1995] PIQR P380.

21 years of age, an accomplished athlete and the risks would have been obvious to a reasonably intelligent person.

The fact that an instructor or coach is very experienced does not mean that a participant can abdicate all personal responsibility and blindly follow an instructor's suggestion. In the case of *Anderson v Lyotier and Portejoie*[24], a ski instructor was held to have failed to take reasonable care in inviting the claimant to ski off-piste without taking the claimant's ability sufficiently into consideration, especially as he was one of the weaker members of the ski group. However, Foskett J warned that it was a collaborative process and the claimant should have voiced his concerns that off piste ski-ing was beyond his capabilities:

> *"In my judgment, if an instructor does suggest something to a skier under his supervision that the skier believes to be beyond what it is reasonable for him to attempt, there is an onus on the skier to say so…I do not consider it is, objectively speaking, reasonable for the skier not to say something in that situation. The human reaction not to want to appear awkward, difficult or, as Mr Foxon put it, "faint-hearted" is quite understandable from a subjective viewpoint; but objective analysis does suggest that serious concerns must be ventilated".*

Therefore, even if a timid participant would prefer to refrain from publicly pointing out their lack of confidence/skill, the court will apply its own, objective, view. The claimant in that case was found to be one-third responsible and ski instructor two-thirds responsible.

Clubs involved in contact sport sometimes ask their players to undertake a cognitive assessment at the beginning of each season in order to assess their cognitive responses after a potential head injury/concussion. If a player is found to have deliberately underperformed in their original cognitive test, in order to minimise the impact of any concussion, they are likely to be found to be contributory negligent.

---

24 [2008] EWHC 2790, [2008] All ER (D) 216 (Nov).

Contributory negligence and children

Courts have recognised that young children are less able to appreciate and assess risks and danger. Accordingly, the courts have adopted a variation of the objective test; they will objectively assess what the reasonable behaviour for a child of a certain age should be.

There is no minimum age threshold for a finding of contributory negligence. The youngest claimant found guilty of contributory negligence was a seven-year-old boy who had punched through a pane of glass at school[25]. Whilst a court will consider all the circumstances of each case, the following factors will be significant:

1. The particular danger involved;
2. The age of that child;
3. The degree of care that would be expected of a child of that age; and
4. The intellectual level of that child.

In *Russell v Smith*[26], a 10 year old cyclist was held to be a vulnerable road user and, therefore, despite the fact he was held to be three-quarters responsible for the accident, it was just and equitable under s.1 Law Reform (Contributory Negligence) Act 1945 to reduce his damages, not in accordance with his share of responsibility for the accident, but by 50 per cent only. The court held there was a high duty on other road users to make allowance for the inexperience and lack of caution of children.

In *C (A Child) v W School*[27], the claimant, who was 17½ at the time of the accident, suffered significant spinal injuries in a ski-ing accident when he decided to ski off-piste. Although the court held that the "*primary cause of the accident*" was that the claimant "*was travelling too*

25 *N (a child) v Newham London Borough Council* [2007] CLY 2931.

26 High Court, 30 July 2003.

27 [2002] P.I.Q.R. P13 (QBD).

fast and out of control, that he failed to pay attention to the topography, the presence of the warning sign and the fact that slower moving skiers were in front of him", the court stated that it was foreseeable that a 17 year old would behave irresponsibly and reasonable steps should have been taken to protect him. The court reduced the claimant's damages by 50%. Clearly, the older the child, the greater the degree of care he or she will be expected to take.

Although almost all cases in England and Wales adopt the objective approach of determining reasonable behaviour for a child of a certain age and holding the claimant to that standard, there have been some cases where a party has contended for a more subjective approach. In *Rheman v Brady*[28] the defendant sought to argue that the particular characteristics of a 7 year old claimant could be taken into account if it put her in a better position than "*an ordinary child of her age*" to appreciate the risks of crossing a road. However, the court gave no real consideration of this argument, stating there was no basis for contributory negligence on the grounds that it was the defendant's speed that caused the accident.

(D) DISCLAIMERS & EXCLUSION CLAUSES

In a number of historic cases, disclaimers or exclusion clauses were effective in limiting or excluding the liability of the defendant. In White v Blackmore,[29] the claimant's husband was killed when watching a jalopy race at the defendant's premises. The deceased had been a competitor in an earlier race and when he had signed on to race had been in the location of notices that warned of the dangers of motor racing and that stated that it was a condition of admission as a spectator that the organisers were absolved of any liability resulting from accidents "howsoever caused". The deceased's family had paid for their admission while the deceased had been admitted for free, as a competitor. The defence of *volenti non fit injuria* failed, however the organisers' liability to the claimant for the death of her husband was

---

28 [2012] EWHC 78 (QB).

29 [1972] 2 QB 651, CA.

successfully excluded by the notices as at the time of his death he was present as a spectator.

While that was the position historically, it now seems unlikely that the same outcome would result if those cases were litigated again in view of the effect of section 2(1) of the Unfair Contract Terms Act 1977, which provides that where operating in the course of a business an individual cannot exclude liability for death or personal injury by means of the terms of a contract or by a notice containing a disclaimer.[30]

Exclusion and limitation clauses remain relevant however in that liability for property damage can be limited or excluded provided that any such exclusion or limitation must be reasonable in the circumstances.[31] Further, in circumstances where an injured claimant brings proceedings against a defendant, who may then seek to pass on any liability that may attach to them to an additional party,[32] then any contractual exclusion or limitation in place between them may yet be effective, depending on the particular circumstances, and so the contractual relationship between potential defendants also warrants consideration.

30 See Bacon v White & Chartfield Associates Limited, May 21, 1998, QBD, LTL 22/5/98 (unreported elsewhere).

31 Section 2(2) UCTA 1977.

32 E.g. joined by virtue of the defendant having made an additional claim within Part 20 of the Civil Procedure Rules.

CHAPTER ELEVEN
DAMAGES

INTRODUCTION

The remedies available to a successful claimant in a successful sports case may be wider than simply an award of damages in that they may include a right to injunctions, declarations or to public law remedies,[1] however in the context of a claim for damages for personal injuries arising from sport the award of damages is usually the most important. The assessment of damages follows the conventional formula that one sees in the non-sports personal injury claim. In this chapter we briefly discuss the available heads of claim generally followed by a more detailed consideration of a number of particular heads of loss which merit closer attention in the sporting context, including claims for the loss of a sporting career based on the anticipated trajectory of the claimant's sporting career, loss of congenial employment claims and the issue of aggravated damages in respect of cases of assault.

HEADS OF LOSS GENERALLY

As with the non-sports personal injury case the heads of loss usually advanced include general damages claims for (i) pain, suffering and loss of amenity, (ii) loss of congenial employment, and (iii) damages for dis-advantage on the labour market, as well as the usual heads of special damages claims including (i) damages in respect of past and future lost earnings or income, (ii) damages for care and assistance, (iii) travel and transport, (iv) past and future treatment and therapy, (v) damaged clothing/possessions, (vi) case management, (vii) equipment, (viii) accommodation, (ix) assistive technology, and (x) court of protection expenses. A full exposition of those heads of damages can be found in other works.[2]

---

1 For further discussion of other remedies in cases other than ones involving personal injury see Beloff et.al., *Sports Law*, second edition, 2012, at 8.12.

2 E.g. see Latimer-Sayer et al., *Personal Injury Schedules: Calculating Damages* (3rd edition, 2010).

LOSS OF CAREER CLAIMS

In the sports law personal injury claim the injured party may be at the beginning of what would otherwise have been a highly successful and lucrative career. The starting point is that the claim for lost earnings or income is advanced in the conventional way with the claimant's loss being calculated by reference to their pre-injury earnings with credit being given for any receipts in the period between the injury and trial, when considering past loss and with credit being given for assumed residual earnings into the future. However, in cases where the claimant's case is that but for the injury his or her career would have taken off or have continued to thrive, the residual earnings must be compared with what the claimant would have achieved but for the breach of duty. That poses particular difficulties of evidence for the claimant in a sports case, who would argue that but for the injury they would have gone on to have achieved further successes, leading to greater levels of public recognition and substantially higher levels of remuneration. Such success and remuneration is usually achieved by way of a combination of talent, hard work and luck when one considers the importance of the need to time training so as to peak at the right time as well as when one considers the good fortune required in avoiding injury, which is a particular risk in both contact and non-contact sports. There are therefore a large number of imponderables for the claimant to seek to remove by way of evidence where possible and which a defendant might point to in order to argue that the claim is based largely on speculation.

The case that the injured claimant has lost their potentially lucrative sporting career may be advanced in two alternative ways. The first involves applying the conventional multiplier / multiplicand approach to a single assumed career model, with concessions being made by way of adjustments to the multiplier and/or to the multiplicand to reflect the imponderables and uncertainties that exist. The second would be to assume a conservative baseline career model and to seek one hundred percent of the damages calculated on that basis, together with further damages to reflect the lost chance of achieving further remuneration associated with any alternative more lucrative career model.[3] Clearly,

3 Applying the principle in Davies v Taylor [1974] AC 207 at 212H-213A.

the loss of a sporting career claim lends itself to the loss of chance approach, given that the claimant's success in their future career will be dependent in part on the actions and decisions of third parties.[4] If a loss of chance approach is appropriate, then it should be immaterial that various contingencies make the assessment difficult or uncertain.[5]

Although not a sports injury case, *Herring v Ministry of Defence*[6] is illustrative of the court's approach in circumstances in which a number of alternative career models may be advanced and which are dependent upon decisions that would have been made by the claimant and third parties. In *Herring* the claimant was injured during a parachuting accident as a result of the defendant's negligence. The claimant's case was that but for the negligence he would have gone on to have had a successful career in the police force on being discharged from the armed forces at the end of his service career. The trial judge found that but for the accident the claimant would have applied for and secured a role in the police force and that he would probably have risen to the rank of sergeant within seven years or alternatively he would have achieved similar employment with a similar level of remuneration. The judge applied a multiplier/multiplicand approach to the calculation but reduced the multiplier by 25% to reflect contingencies. On appeal the Court of Appeal observed that the assessment of future loss of earnings had not traditionally involved a loss of a chance assessment based on the likely actions of third parties, save in exceptional circumstances. They acknowledged that the traditional approach was to adjust the multiplier or multiplicand to reflect the prospect of increases in earnings or in respect of any other relevant contingencies or vicissitudes. It was confirmed that where the career model adopted by the trial judge was an appropriate baseline or was one of a number of alternative career models which were all likely to result in the same or a similar outcome, it was not necessary to adopt the percentage chance approach. The Court of Appeal concluded however that the 25% reduction was too great to reflect the prospect of the claimant not achieving the career model

4 See Allied Maple Group v Simmons & Simmons [1995] 1 WLR 1602.

5 Chaplin v Hicks [1911] 2 KB 786 per Vaughan Williams LJ at 791-2.

6 Herring v Ministry of Defence [2003] EWCA Civ 528.

adopted. It was observed that in order to justify greater reductions than those provided for in the notes to the Ogden Tables there should be tangible reasons relating to the particular circumstances of the claimant beyond the simply speculative.

Accordingly, if the alternative career models are unlikely to result in a large difference in the value of the claims based on each set of assumptions then the court may decline to apply a loss of chance approach and simply prefer one career model over another, adjusting the calculation as appropriate to take account of the contingencies. However, it also follows that in circumstances where the alternative career model envisages and assumes particular success in a sport, with a substantial difference in remuneration as between that and what might be considered a safe or conservative baseline assumption, then the court is likely to make a separate assessment of that further loss on a loss of chance basis, provided that there is sufficient evidence to take that approach.[7]

In the case of *Brown v Ministry of Defence*,[8] the favourable pension terms available to a service woman who was injured shortly after enlisting but who was held to have been someone who would probably have remained in the military for a full 22-year career were sufficient circumstances to justify adopting an approach involving the separate assessment of her loss of pension rights on a percentage prospects basis. The judge at first instance had awarded the claimant her full loss of pension rights having adopted an all or nothing basis. The Court of Appeal assessed her pension entitlement as being the sum of (a) one hundred percent of the value of the Claimant's pension rights had she served for six years, (b) fifty percent of the additional value of the

7 In Lyon v Ministry of Defence, 31 Mar 2011, Leicester CC, Recorder Potts, LTL 13/9/11, the court adopted a lump sum award in respect of one phase of the career model advanced by the claimant as the uncertainties were considered too great to adopt an alternative approach, applying Blamire v South Cumbria Health Authority [1993] PIQR Q1. Further, in Dixon v Were [2004] EWHC 2273, part of the claimant's claim that he suffered the lost opportunity to earn very large sums as an accountant was rejected where the claimant was injured while still a student at university.

8 [2006] EWCA Civ 546, [2006] PIQR Q9.

claimant's pension rights had she served for twelve years, and (c) thirty percent of the additional value of the claimant's pension rights had she served for twenty two years. While *Brown* was not a sports injury case, specific reference was made in the judgment to the loss of chance approach being appropriate in cases in which a sportsman might advance a claim for the loss of a lucrative career.[9]

Turning to cases decided in the context of the injured sportsperson, in *Langford v Hebran*,[10] the claimant was a world champion kick-boxer who suffered injury in a road traffic collision. Prior to the accident the claimant had worked as a trainee bricklayer for five months while his career as a kick-boxer was taking off. He had been an amateur world champion and at the time of the accident had won his first professional fight. He was predicted to become a world champion professional fighter and to go on to become a kick-boxing instructor on retirement. Adopting the principles applied in *Doyle v Wallace,*[11] a case in which the claimant lost the chance of a teaching career, the trial judge assessed the claimant's future loss of earnings claim based upon: (1) the full value of a claim which assumed that the claimant would have become a professional fighter and teacher for nine years, during which time he would have continued to work as a part-time bricklayer and following which he would have reverted to bricklaying to the age of 60 years, together with (2) percentage awards in respect of the income differentials associated with four alternative career scenarios as a kick-boxer and instructor to reflect the prospect of each career path being achieved, with each scenario being dependent on the claimant having achieved the previous scenario. The claimant was awarded £326,370 by way of damages for his future loss of earnings with the judge having assessed the chances of him achieving each of the alternative scenarios as (a) twenty percent, (b) forty percent, (c) thirty percent and (d) ten percent.

---

9 Citing Robert Langford v (1) Gary Hebran (2) Nynex Cablecomms [2001] EWCA Civ 361, [2001] PIQR Q160.

10 Ibid, cited with approval in in Clarke v Maltby [2010] EWHC 1201 (QB), XYZ v Portsmouth Hospitals NHS Trust [2011] EWHC 243 (QB), (2011) 121 BLMR 13 and in Tait v Gloucestershire Hospitals NHS Foundation Trust [2015] EWHC 848 (QB).

11 (1998) PIQR P146.

On appeal the Court of Appeal concluded that the trial judge had applied too high a multiplicand in respect of the claimant's likely earnings as an instructor and that the percentage chance of scenario (a) could not be smaller than the percentage chance of scenario (b) as the claimant would have had to have achieved scenario (a) in order to go on to achieve scenario (b). The Court of Appeal re-assessed the prospects of the alternative scenarios as (a) eighty percent, (b) sixty six percent, (c) forty percent, and (d) twenty percent but as the overall total award on those assumptions was not substantially different to the sum in fact awarded by the trial judge the Court of Appeal did not interfere with the award made at first instance.

Another helpful case to consider is *Appleton v El Safty*.[12] In that case the claimant sought damages from the defendant surgeon arising from negligent treatment, which included damages in respect of the loss of his footballing career. At the time of the surgery in 2001 and aged 26 years, the claimant had been playing as a central midfielder for a premiership team. The claimant suffered a partially torn anterior cruciate ligament in training and rather than advising conservative management the defendant advised the claimant to have reconstruction surgery, which was then negligently performed. As a consequence the claimant required further surgery and ultimately suffered the loss of his footballing career. The evidence indicated that had he been conservatively treated the claimant would have been able to return to professional football by April 2002. The court concluded that but for the negligence the claimant was likely to have remained under contract with the premiership club until at least June 2005 at which point there was a seventy five percent chance of him continuing at championship level for two years and a twenty five percent chance of him continuing at division one level. The evidence also indicated that at that point it was likely that the claimant would have had to retire from professional football. The claimant's claims for loss of salary, bonuses, loyalty payments, fringe benefits, media and sponsorship opportunities were assessed on those assumptions. A claim was also made for the lost opportunity of pursuing a football management career. Although the court concluded that the chances of the claimant pursuing that latter

12 Michael Appleton v Medhat Mohammed El Safty [2007] EWHC 631 (QB).

role were remote and there were difficulties in (a) estimating the chances of securing such a role and (b) as to the period that he might remain in such a role, such that they rendered the exercise close to speculation, nevertheless the court considered that it would be unjust to make no award at all in view of the evidence of the claimant's coaching aptitude and dedication and awarded him a lump sum of £60,000 under that head of claim.

In *Collett v Smith*,[13] the claimant was a member of a premiership football club's youth academy who suffered a significant leg injury due to a negligent tackle. He was playing his first game for the club's adult reserve team at the age of eighteen. As a consequence the claimant did not regain his previous level of fitness and his career was brought to an end. The claim included one for the loss of his footballing career. The trial judge assessed the future loss of earnings (1) by beginning with a conservative assumption that the claimant would have played throughout his career for at least a championship league club, then (2) by applying a twenty five percent increase to the average earnings of such a player to reflect the evidence that he would at least have played in a club at the upper end of the championship league, then (3) by applying an annual increase in earnings of fifteen percent based on a survey of earnings to reflect the actual increase in earnings received by players in the championship league in 2007-2008 and 2008-2009, and then (4) by applying a fifteen percent discount to the overall award to reflect contingencies including, for example, the risk of injury in any event. On appeal the first defendant contended that the trial judge should have adopted a loss of chance approach to the assessment and that the fifteen percent reduction was too low. The Court of Appeal dismissed the appeal on the basis that the evidence that the claimant would at least have played for a championship league team and one at the upper end of that league was strong and that the judge had not failed to take into account the possibility of the claimant not achieving that position. Rather she had considered the possibility to be small and had taken account of it along with other contingencies, including pre-

13 Benjamin Collett v (1) Gary Smith (2) Middlesbrough Football & Athletics Company (1986) Ltd [2009] EWCA Civ 583 and [2008] EWHC 1962 (QB), cited with approval in XYZ v Portsmouth Hospitals NHS Trust [2011] EWHC 243(QB), (2011) 121 BMLR 13.

mature termination for other reasons. The assessment and in particular the level of the reduction that was applied of fifteen percent from the assumed career path also took into account the possibility that the claimant might have done better than the assumptions made by the court including the prospect of the claimant spending part of his career playing for a premiership club.[14]

These provide a helpful illustration of how such a claim might be advanced. A claimant would be well advised to seek as much evidence as they can to support as generous a baseline as possible, in addition to clear evidence that confirms the extent of their skill and ability, so that the court is in a position to assess the extent of the chance of them achieving success at the highest level.

DAMAGES FOR LOSS OF CONGENIAL EMPLOYMENT

The award of damages for loss of congenial employment has been awarded for decades and is intended to compensate for the loss of the particular enjoyment that the claimant derived from their work. In the case of the injured sports person it is usually not difficult for a claimant to get over the threshold of recovery, with the courts generally accepted that sports bring with them pleasure for the participant as well as remuneration in the case of the professional. While these awards were initially made to employees in public sector roles such as nursing, fire and police services,[15] the circumstances in which such award have been made are now much wider. The suggestion that such awards are confined to particular categories of employment has been expressly rejected.[16]

---

14 The discount applied to the overall award for contingencies at the end as applied in *Collett* has been adopted in a number of cases more recently, including in XYZ v Portsmouth Hospitals NHS Trust [2011] EWHC 243 (QB) (loss of income from business) but not in others, e.g. see Clarke v Maltby [2010] EWHC 1201 (QB) (loss of career as solicitor).

15 E.g. Leatherland v Edwards, 28 Oct 1998, QBD, Lawtel 23/1/99.

16 Pratt v Smith, unreported, 18 Dec 2002, QBD and see also *Loss of Congenial Employment*, Simon Allen, JPIL 2009, 2, 135-139.

Where it is accepted that the nature of the employment in question can be taken to have been inherently enjoyable and sufficient evidence of their actual enjoyment pre-injury has been advanced by the claimant, awards have been made under this head but they have generally been limited to sums of up to £10,000-£15,000.[17] Exceptionally larger awards have been made in sporting cases in which clear and cogent evidence of a loss of particular enjoyment and prestige may be available, as in *Appleton v El Safty*,[18] in which an award was made under this head of £25,000.

However, in cases in which the sporting career has not yet begun and the loss of a sporting career is advanced on a loss of chance basis, with the baseline award being an assumption that the claimant would not have achieved a sporting career, then it is unlikely that any award would be made under this head.[19]

As regards evidence in relation to such a head of claim, given the sizeable award made in *Appleton*, the claimant would be sensible to take the time to collect and advance evidence dealing specifically with the loss of enjoyment point, including examples to fully illustrate what has been lost.

LOSS OF OPPORTUNITY TO COMPETE

A possible further award of general damages that may be available to the sportsperson is an award to represent the lost opportunity to compete in prestigious competitions and tournaments. In *Mulvaine v Joseph*,[20] the plaintiff was an American professional golfer visiting the UK for the purpose of competing in seven golfing tournaments. He suffered injury to his left hand as a result of the negligence of a taxi driver and was awarded £1,000 by way of damages for the lost opportunity to compete in five tournaments and the loss of experience and prestige, although

17 In Langford (citation above) a not untypical sum of £7,500 was awarded, whereas in Leatherland v Edwards (citation above) the award was £3,000.

18 Appleton v El Safty [2007] EWHC 631 (QB).

19 See Moody v Aviva & another, 26/12/2010, Kingston upon Hull County Court, reported LTL 4/5/2011.

20 (1968) 112 SJ 927, (1968) 118 NLJ 1078.

some element of that lump sum general damages award was intended to compensate for the lost chance of winning prize money.

REHABILITATION COSTS

In the non-sports personal injury claim one commonly sees claims for the cost of rehabilitation, that is the cost of assisting the injured person to regain their pre-accident level of physical and/or mental function. It is worth bearing in mind that in the sports law context the claim for damages in relation to the cost of rehabilitation should include the additional cost of rehabilitating the sports person back to their pre-accident level of fitness, despite the fact that that may involve them being rehabilitated to a greater than average level of function. The tort-feasor must take their victim as they find them and the cost of rehabilitating the injured sportsperson to their pre-accident fitness might or should be seen as a step taken in mitigation of what might otherwise be a much greater loss of career claim. It is therefore important to consider in such a claim not simply the cost of rehabilitating the sportsperson back to health, but rather the additional cost of rehabilitating them back to their pre-accident level of function and fitness and to collect evidence to demonstrate what may well be a substantially greater level of professional input.

AGGRAVATED AND EXEMPLARY DAMAGES

As discussed above, the aim of damages are to compensate the claimant for a wrong. They are designed to remedy, so far as possible, the pecuniary or non-pecuniary loss suffered by the victim by putting him or her into as good a position as if no wrong had occurred[21]. Therefore, general damages for pain suffering and loss of amenity broadly compensate a claimant for the immediate and long term impact of the actual tort. The amount payable is usually calculated by reference to a tariff system, the Judicial College's 'Guidelines for the Assessment of General Damages in Personal Injury Cases'.

However, aggravated and exemplary damages go further than this; they are two major types of 'exceptional' damages. They allow the court to

---

21 *Livingstone v Rawyards Coal Co.* (1880) 5 AC 25, *per* Lord Blackburn at 39.

take account of the manner in which the tort is committed. A simple way of differentiating them is to say that aggravated damages are awarded for behaviour that shocks the claimant whereas exemplary damages are awarded for behaviour which shocks the court. Whilst aggravated damages are solely compensatory, they are usually higher than what a claimant would normally receive. Exemplary damages are punitive.

In the sports context, it is envisaged that increased importance will be placed on damages falling outside the usual categories. Aggravated damages will, especially, be a useful tool to increase the amount of compensation available. Whilst there is ample exposition of damages for pain, pain suffering and loss of amenity in legal commentary and writings, the area of aggravated damages and exemplary damages has sometimes attracted confusion about their function and applicability[22]. Given their likely increase importance in the future, it is proposed to provide a brief outline in the principles governing these exceptional damages.

Function of aggravated damages

In recent years, courts have shown themselves to be more open to awarding aggravated damages. Although there is some uncertainty about the exact definition and function of aggravated damages, the leading case on aggravated damages, *Rookes v Barnard*[23], suggests that aggravated damages may be awarded to compensate a claimant for mental distress, or injury to feelings, in circumstances in which that injury has been caused or increased by the manner in which the defendant committed the wrong.

In essence, the defendant's motives, conduct or manner of inflicting the injury may have aggravated the claimant's damage by injuring his or her feelings of dignity and pride. Such motive, conduct or manner 'aggravates' the injury which therefore warrants an additional compensatory sum.

---

22 This confusion has been recognised by the Law Commission in its paper *'Aggravated, Exemplary and Restitutionary Damages'*, 16 December 1997, LC247.

23 [1964] UKHL 1

In *Thompson and another v Commissioner of Police of the Metropolis*[24] Lord Woolf MR gave as examples in cases involving misdeeds committed by police officers:

> *"... humiliating circumstances at the time of arrest or any conduct of those responsible for the arrest or the prosecution which shows that they had behaved in a high handed, insulting, malicious or oppressive manner either in relation to the arrest or imprisonment or in conducting the prosecution."*

Further, Lord Woolf MR outlined the function of aggravated damages:

> *'. . .the distinction between basic and aggravated damages will continue to have a part to play as long as the right to recover for intangible consequences such as humiliation, injury to pride and dignity as well as for the hurt caused by the spiteful, malicious, insulting or arrogant conduct of the defendant attaches to some causes of action and not others.'*

When will aggravated damages be awarded?

Case law suggests there are two basic preconditions of an award of aggravated damages[25]:

(1) exceptional or contumelious conduct or motive on the part of a defendant in committing the wrong, or, in certain circumstances, subsequent to the wrong; and

(2) mental distress sustained by the claimant as a result.

When assessing aggravated damages, courts are entitled to take account of a defendant's conduct after the tort and leading up to trial. Therefore, should the defendant impugn the claimant's character leading up to trial, this could be viewed as conduct designed to aggravate the injury.

---

24 [1997] EWCA Civ 104

25 Law Commission, '*Aggravated, Exemplary and Restitutionary Damages*', 16 December 1997, LC247.

The claimant must be actually aware of the defendant's exceptional motive or conduct; otherwise there can be no aggravating injury to feelings.

Overlap between aggravated damages and damages for pain, suffering and loss of amenity

Authorities are not always consistent as to whether aggravated damages should be assessed separately from pain, suffering and loss of amenity or whether a single increased award should be made.

In the case of *Richardson v Howie*[26], it was decided that, in an assault case, damages for injury to feelings should be awarded as general rather than aggravated damages, i.e. there should be no separate award for aggravated damages: whilst it was "*…appropriate to compensate for injury to feelings including the indignity, mental suffering, humiliation or distress that might be caused by such an attack, as well as anger or indignation arising from the circumstances of the attack…* [the] *court should not characterise the award of damages for injury to feelings… as aggravated damages"*.

In *Martins v Choudhary*[27], the Court of Appeal refused an invitation to follow a previous recommendation of the court in *Richardson v Howie* that single global awards should be made in assault cases and stated that *"there should be no hard and fast rule about whether separate awards should be made. It all depends on the facts of the individual case. If, for example, as is sometimes the case, the psychiatric harm is very modest and to all intents and purposes merges with the injury to feelings, it will plainly be more convenient to make on award covering both aspects. If, as here, where the psychiatric injury is not insubstantial, it is positively helpful to the parties (and to this Court) if the judge separates the award for psychiatric injury from that for injury to feelings. This leads to a better understanding of the judge's thought processes. However, I do accept that there is a risk of double recovery by overlap if two awards are made and the judge must take care to avoid that."* (at paragraph 18). It is therefore arguable that if

26 [2005] PIQR Q3 CA.

27 [2007] EWCA Civ 1379.

there are identifiable aggravating features in a claim it remains proper to make a separate award for the aggravating damages.

The approach of *Richardson v Howie* was also qualified in *AB and Others (JA, JPM, RM)*[28], where Irwin J addressed the general approach to awarding damages for sexual abuse. He preferred the approach outlined by the Court of Appeal in *Martins v Choudhary*, i.e. the avoidance of any hard and fast rule as to whether separate awards should be made for psychiatric harm, injury to feelings and aggravated damages. Irwin J concluded *"Therefore the approach I adopt in a case where no discrete psychiatric disorder is demonstrated, is to consider the adverse psychiatric consequences as part of the picture to be borne in mind when considering the level of damages at large for the assault itself."*

McGregor on Damages (19th ed) also questions the approach in *Richardson v Howie* and makes this point that *"the classification of aggravated damages as compensatory does not mean that one is not independent of the other and that the one should be subsumed within the other. If the scale or the horror of the assault increases the injury to the Claimant's feelings, the damage is aggravated, and hence the damages are aggravated, and the courts have recognised this in their awards."*

It is of note that the definition of aggravated damages in the Civil Procedure Rules 2016 is '*additional damages which the court may award as compensation for the defendant's objectionable behaviour*' (emphasis added).

What type of case attracts aggravated damages?

Aggravated damages are *usually* only available for wrongs which are actionable *per se*, i.e. not limited to the pecuniary loss that can be specifically proved. However, so far as personal injury is concerned, they are only available in cases of trespass against the person and other intentional torts. In cases of pure negligence, no award of aggravated damages is recoverable: *Kralj v McGrath*[29].

---

28 [2010] EWHC 1005.

29 [1986] 1 All ER 54 at 60–61, [1985] NLJ Rep 913 at 913 per Woolf J.

The reasoning of Woolf J in *Kralj v McGrath* was as follows:

> *"it would be wholly inappropriate to introduce into claims of this sort, for breach of contract and negligence, the concept of aggravated damages. If it were to apply in this situation of a doctor not treating a patient in accordance with his duty, whether under contract or in tort, then I would consider that it must apply in other situations where a person is under a duty to exercise care. It would be difficult to see why it could not even extend to cases where damages are brought for personal injuries in respect of driving. If the principle is right, a higher award of damages would be appropriate in a case of reckless driving which caused injury than would be appropriate in cases where careless driving caused identical injuries. Such a result seems to me to be wholly inconsistent with the general approach to damages in this area, which is to compensate the plaintiff for the loss that she has actually suffered, so far as it is possible to do so, by the award of monetary compensation and not to treat those damages as being a matter which reflects the degree of negligence or breach of duty of the defendant."*

The reasoning of Woolf J was applied in *AB v South West Water Services*[30] where the court stated the claimants could not claim aggravated damages for their anger and indignation at the Defendants' high-handed conduct because the claimants could only claim compensatory damages, and anger and indignation were not proper subjects for compensatory damages (despite them being proper subjects for aggravated damages in assault and battery cases).

However, the reasoning of Woolf J is 30 years old and has attracted criticism. The Law Commission has stated that whilst *Kralj* and *AB* stand as modern authorities to the effect that aggravated damages are unavailable for the tort of negligence, "*it is unfortunately not easy to understand the justification for this restriction*" and it has not been possible to "*detect any good reason*" for such a restriction. The law in this regard may change in future. This is especially the case in the sports context where professional relationships with vulnerable and young athletes can be exploited to further the professional's own motives or where

30 [1993] QB 507, [1993] 1 All ER 609, CA.

a dangerous tackle was made in circumstances where it does not amount to an assault but was executed with a view to gaining an advantage on the field.

Aggravated damages in sports law

There are a number of factors which could influence the imposition of aggravated damages in the sports law context. A court may be influenced by the fact that the tort was broadcast as part of the game or committed in public, or calculated to injure the most talented player in the opposite team.

There have been no reported cases in the UK on the imposition of aggravated damages for personal injury in the sporting context. However, in the Australian case of *Canterbury Bankstown Rugby Football League Club Ltd v Rogers; Bugden v Rogers*[31], aggravated damages were imposed where a deliberate assault took place, by an opposing player, live on national television. In the employment context, aggravated damages are well established and may provide helpful comparators for setting the level. There are many notable cases of aggravated damages being awarded to athletes where it was shown they were discriminated against: Dr Eva Carneiro sought aggravated damages for sex discrimination by Jose Mourinho in her claim, settled in June 2016[32].

EXEMPLARY DAMAGES

Exemplary damages is a concept developed under the common law. Whereas aggravated damages compensate the claimant for injury to feelings when his or her distress was exacerbated by the circumstances in which the injury was caused or by the conduct of the defendant, the aim of exemplary damages is to punish the defendant.

A court can only award exemplary damages where the facts fall into one of the two "categories" of wrongful act where they are available, unless exemplary damages are provided for by statute. The two categories are:

---

31 [1993] Aust Tort Reports 81-246.

32 https://www.theguardian.com/football/2016/jun/07/jose-mourinho-unexpectedly-turns-up-at-employment-tribunal-eva-carneiro.

1. oppressive, arbitrary or unconstitutional action by a public servant, or

2. where the defendant's wrongful conduct was calculated to make a profit which might well exceed the compensation payable to the claimant.

Most personal injury claims in sports law will not fall within the first category, although "public servants" have be should be "widely construed" to include anyone exercising governmental power[33].

However, there may well be cases were a club or organisation commits a tort in a manner calculated to increase its profit. In this context, "profit" can be extended as a definition "beyond money making" in the strict sense[34]. It could include covering up a tort to prevent future loss of sponsorship or income[35].

Again, there are no reported cases in the UK on the imposition of exemplary damages for personal injury in the sporting context. In the case of *Bugden v Rogers*, noted above, the claimant alleged he had been deliberately targeted and injured by the defendant as part of a specific in-game strategy put forward by the coach of the opposing team. Although this allegation was not proved, the court indicated that had it found there was a deliberate plan to injury players on the oppsting team, it would have imposed exemplary damages of around of A$150,000. This equated to over double the amount awarded as special and general damages. This is not surprising given the purpose of exemplary damages.

---

33 Broome v Cassell & Co Ltd [1972] AC 1027.

34 *Rookes v Barnard* [1964] AC 1129, per Lord Devlin.

35 *Catnic Components Ltd v Hill* [1983] FSR 512: a case involving sexual abuse at a school which was covered up in order to prevent losing future school fees if it was disclosed.

CHAPTER TWELVE
EXPERT EVIDENCE

INTRODUCTION

In this short chapter we consider the areas in which expert evidence is usually required in sports law cases. It discusses the need for and uses of expert evidence in relation to issues of breach of duty, causation and the quantum of damages and also the procedural requirements to consider during the process of commissioning such evidence and in relation to obtaining permission to rely on such evidence.

THE NEED FOR EXPERT EVIDENCE

When is expert evidence required?

Expert evidence is generally appropriate where the issues include a consideration of matters outside of the knowledge of the court and which cannot simply be assumed, with judicial notice being taken of that matter or which cannot be gleaned from the factual evidence. In those circumstances the opinion of an expert is required. The court has considered the circumstances in which expert evidence may be called upon as being (a) where the expert evidence is necessary in the sense that an issue cannot be decided without it, and (b) where the issue can be determined without expert evidence but the court will be assisted by the opinion of an expert.[1]

Duty of care and breach of duty

Examples of areas in which one can expect a court to be willing to look to expert evidence for guidance in the sporting context, would include, in relation to breach of duty (i) where consideration is required at the duty of care and breach of duty stages of what is normal for the sport, in terms of the risks that participants know that they are running; (ii) as to the usual safety measures taken by taken organisers and promoters;

---

1 British Airways plc v Paul Spencer and others (Present Trustees of the Airways Pension Scheme) [2015] EWHC 2477 (Ch), Warren J. at paragraph 61-63 and 68.

(iii) as to a sporting governing body's or licensing authority's safety guidelines and as to how they are usually implemented in practice; or (iv) where, in a sports physician case, a consideration is required of whether the medical management provided by the physician fell below that of a responsible body of sports physicians.

Factual and medical causation

One can also see that medical experts will be required to give evidence as to factual causation, i.e. describing as a matter of fact what medical management was appropriate instead of that which was provided and as to medical causation, i.e. as to what the medical consequences of failing to provide the necessary and appropriate management were.

Quantum of damages

Similarly, as in any other personal injury action, when considering quantum medical evidence will be required that deals fully with the injured claimant's condition, treatment and prognosis. Such evidence may be from medical experts in a wide range of disciplines including orthopaedics, psychiatry, neurosurgery, general surgery and physiotherapy, to identify just a small selection. In cases of greater severity, expert evidence that supports (or rebuts) the need for care and case management, aids and equipment, physiotherapy, occupational therapy, speech and language therapy, accommodation, assistive technology and court of protection costs in cases in which the injured claimant lacks capacity, may also be required.

In the case of the claim alleging the loss of what would otherwise have been a very successful sporting career, it will be imperative for the claimant to obtain detailed evidence from an employment expert to deal with (a) the injured claimant's likely and possible career trajectories had there been no injury, for the purposes of advancing a loss of earnings claim possibly based on a loss of chance assessment, and (b) what, if any, residual earning capacity the claimant now has.

PROCEDURAL CONSIDERATIONS

The Personal Injury Pre-Action Protocol

When bringing any claim for damages for personal injuries the parties' representatives ought to have regard to the personal injury pre-action protocol, introduced with the Civil Procedure Rules from April 1999.[2] While it was envisaged that the protocol would apply to lower value claims likely to be allocated to the fast track the protocol provides that the "cards on the table" approach advocated by the protocol applies equally to cases of higher value and that in multi-track cases the spirit if not the letter of the protocol should be complied with.[3] From the perspective of obtaining expert evidence the protocol suggests that the parties should in the first instance jointly select experts unless the case is likely to be allocated to the multi-track. That is not a joint instruction but involves the claimant nominating experts and the defendant being given the opportunity of objecting to the instruction of that expert before the claimant proceeds to commissioning a report from them.[4] Where the defendant objects to all of the claimant's preferred experts then the parties are at liberty to instruct their own and the court will determine at the end of the case whether the instruction was reasonable or not.[5] Where the defendant does not object to the instruction of an expert the defendant may not rely on its own expert evidence unless the claimant agrees, the court directs or the claimant's expert's report has been amended and the claimant is not willing to disclose the original report.[6]

In most personal injury cases which are likely to be allocated to the multi-track the claimant usually commissions an initial medical report at an early stage without the defendant's involvement, serves that report with the particulars of claim and seeks permission to rely on that report and to obtain further reports, as appropriate, at the first case man-

2 Reproduced in full in the White Book 2016, Vol. 1, C2-001 at p.2381.

3 Paragraph 1.1.2.

4 Paragraph 7.2.

5 Paragraph 7.7.

6 Paragraph 7.8.

agement conference. Clearly, in cases where particular expertise is required in order to enable the claimant to plead the case fully[7] then one can expert the claimant to commission their own report in respect of breach and possibly causation, before proceedings are served, but to hold disclosure of such reports back until the appropriate point in the life of the case.

CPR Part 35 and Permission

By r.35.1 of the Civil Procedure Rules the court has a duty to restrict expert evidence to that which is reasonably required to resolve the proceedings[8] and by CPR r.35.4(1) the court's permission is required to rely on expert evidence.[9] Such permission is usually sought at the first case management conference following the filing of directions questionnaires at which point the claimant usually seeks permission to rely on the expert evidence already obtained and served with proceedings and consideration is then given to what if any further expert evidence may be reasonably required.

The approach of the court since the overriding objective[10] of the Civil Procedure Rules was amended in April 2013 to place particular emphasis on the need for proceedings to be pursued in a way that is proportionate to the amount of sums at stake has been much more restrictive when considering the question of whether to grant permission for expert evidence.

As indicated above, the court usually approaches the question of what is reasonably required by asking whether the expert evidence is necessary, in the sense that an issue in the case cannot be decided without it, and if the issue or issues to which the expert evidence may be relevant can be determined without the expert evidence, the court may then consider whether it would nevertheless be assisted by having such expert evidence

7 E.g. in the sports physician case, expert evidence will be required that supports any allegations of professional negligence being made in the particulars of claim, well before the case is pleaded.

8 See White Book 2016, Vol. 1 at 1020.

9 Ibid at 1025.

10 CPR r.1.1, White Book, Vol. 1 at 9.

available at the trial of the case. In cases where expert evidence is not deemed necessary but may be considered of assistance the court will consider the issue of whether obtaining such evidence is proportionate to the case, taking account of the overriding objective and in particular considerations such as the likely cost of the evidence, the value of the claim, the effect of a judgment either way on the parties, who is to pay for the expert evidence and any delay that obtaining the expert evidence might cause.[11] Additional considerations may include the timing of the application for permission and the importance of the case not only to the parties but also to the public at large.

Accordingly, at the point at which a case is first being prepared, full consideration should be given to the nature of any expert evidence that may be required in the case and where it is considered that expert evidence may not be *absolutely necessary* to determine an issue, whether the expense of obtaining such expert evidence can be justified as being proportionate by reference to the particular features of the case. If it cannot be justified as being proportionate then there is a real risk that permission may not be granted to rely on such expert evidence, even where such evidence has already been obtained.

---

11 See British Airways plc v Paul Spencer and others (Present Trustees of the Airways Pension Scheme) [2015] EWHC 2477 (Ch), Warren J. at paragraph 61-63 and 68.

www.ingramcontent.com/pod-product-compliance
Ingram Content Group UK Ltd.
Pitfield, Milton Keynes, MK11 3LW, UK
UKHW020147290926
15471UKWH00004B/733

9 781911 035046